GW00372990

1

About the Book

Clearly illustrated, with enough detailed technical data for comparisons, this practical reference book is useful for those who know about bikes and those who wish to learn about them. The world's manufacturers are listed alphabetically by name and country and a cross-section of their popular road-going models can be found arranged in engine size order. In trying to capture a genuinely international representation, from a market dominated by a few, very large Japanese manufacturers, it has been necessary to select from the extensive range of machines currently available.

This sixth edition concentrates on the 1987 models and describes, in most instances, motorcycles with UK or European specifications. Because two-wheel road-users share a unique experience and have much in common, the book includes some mopeds and scooters but the emphasis is on the full road-going motorcycle range of each company. Bikes which are not intended for street use are left out of this book, but readers will be able to find a selection of dual purpose trail or enduro machines which can be ridden on road and across country. A brief explanation on the technical specification, given for each model, will be found at the front of the book.

About the Author

Robert Croucher writes about motorcycles because he enjoys riding them, he is fascinated by the history of their development, he is intrigued by the ingenuity of design that goes into their manufacture and he admires the daring of those who race them. In short, he likes the world of biking! A riding experience that included many miles on Hondas, a Ducati and several BMWs has led him to the conviction that the roadcraft skills and understanding that come with regular biking are excellent foundations for all road-users.

He believes that this book will have served a purpose if it settles an argument between enthusiasts over model differences, if it conveys a clear picture of the variety of motorcycles available to the rider around the world today or it inspires the reader to look more closely at what biking can offer as an experience in a mobile, yet energy and safety-conscious society.

The *Observer's* series was launched in 1937 with the publication of *The Observer's Book of Birds*. Today, fifty years later, paperback *Observers* continue to offer practical, useful information on a wide range of subjects, and with every book regularly revised by experts, the facts are right up-to-date. Students, amateur enthusiasts and professional organisations alike will find the latest *Observers* invaluable.

'Thick and glossy, briskly informative' – *The Guardian*

'If you are a serious spotter of any of the things the series deals with, the books must be indispensable' – *The Times Educational Supplement*

MOTORCYCLES

Robert Croucher

FREDERICK WARNE

FREDERICK WARNE

Published by the Penguin Group
27 Wrights Lane, London W8 5TZ, England
Viking Penguin Inc., 40 West 23rd Street, New York, New York 10010, USA
Penguin Books Australia Ltd, Ringwood, Victoria, Australia
Penguin Books Canada Ltd, 2801 John Street, Markham, Ontario, Canada L3R 1B4
Penguin Books (NZ) Ltd, 182–190 Wairau Road, Auckland 10, New Zealand

Penguin Books Ltd, Registered Offices: Harmondsworth, Middlesex, England

First published 1976
Sixth edition 1988

Originally published as *The Observer's Book of Motorcycles* in small hardback
format

ISBN 0 7232 3535 X

Typeset, printed and bound in Great Britain by
William Clowes Limited,
Beccles and London

Introduction to the Sixth Edition

Never before have motorcyclists been offered such a wide range of machines as are currently available from the world's manufacturers. Across most of the world, excepting notably the Eastern Bloc and India, the big four Japanese manufacturers, Honda, Kawasaki, Suzuki and Yamaha, dominate the bike market. Given the present fierce competition for sales, they have chosen to make ever more advanced designs their main selling strategy. The result is a marketing race which presents the biker with frequent model changes and a dazzling display of go-faster technology. Some bikers feel this choice may be destroying the very nature of motorcycling. Motorcyclists have a commitment, almost a relationship with their machines, which the current fully-enclosed, hi-tech road-racers cannot easily match. They have become expensive, too complex for home mechanics and require skilled and regular maintenance to keep them in peak tune. At the top end of the market, the reliability and total performance of the Super Sports machines almost insulates the rider from the act of motorcycling. Their adrenalin-pumping performance and racy looks may be strong on images of power, but they are not so practical for every day biking. The popularity of models such as Honda's XBR500 or Yamaha's SRX600 and the public demand to re-introduce the BMW flat-twins, dropped in favour of the hi-tech K-models, are some recognition that what bikers really want is a return to the traditional motorcycling values of simplicity and economy.

In Europe trail bikes are more popular than road-going sports models and every manufacturer now includes an extensive range of dual-purpose machines in their range. The trend has been to large capacity, single cylinder four-strokes with styling heavily influenced by the big saddle tanks and rear monoshock suspension favoured by the Paris–Dakar Rally teams. Models like Kawasaki's KLR650 or Cagiva's 750 Lucky Explorer were considered big for these machines, until the BMW R100GS arrived to become the world's largest standard production enduro bike. The virtues of these bikes mean they spend much of their time on the road and this has led manufacturers such as Honda, with its Transalp 600V model, to create so-called 'concept' bikes which combine dramatic off-road styling with low weight and torquey engines to make a very practicable touring package.

Custom bikes, modelled on the American Harley-Davidson range, have become even more popular, in particular with the Japanese manufacturers who embellish radical styling with technology and masses of polished chrome and buffed aluminium. Kawasaki's VN1500 Vulcan goes beyond any Harley to claim title to being the world's largest capacity vee-twin. The characteristic Stateside styling comes into its own when bikes are being bought more for their posing qualities at week-ends rather than for their usefulness as cheap, travel-to-work transport.

Despite the wide choices open to bikers, the level of sales in Europe and North America remains disappointing and well below the post-war peaks of the late Fifties and Seventies. Explanations for it blame discriminatory legislation such as the complex learner arrangements in many countries, high rates of unemployment especially amongst young people, the widespread availability of cars which are as cheap to run as most of today's bikes, safety scares, the threat of even greater restrictive measures like compulsory leg-shields and, at times, the weather! The decline in the motorcycle market is clearly on a world-wide scale and, with a few exceptions, this may suggest that either the machines being designed are not what are wanted or that attitudes generally to biking are changing.

A fast-changing model range with eye-catching, race-proved technology and ever more startling performance, may seem to be one way to woo back the bikers, but the real challenge seems to be in attracting the young to two wheels and then keeping them there. One marketing approach that might work involves creative financing with buy-back deals. This would guarantee second-hand values and enable first-time buyers to trade up, once they are experienced, for a larger capacity model. It would also allow the manufacturer to look for, and expect, continued brand loyalty from bikers.

In 1984 several of the smaller motorcycle concerns were forced to cease trading because of falling bike sales. Since then the recession has been weathered by manufacturers reducing production (down 30% in Japan) and cutting back on the range of models offered. To by-pass the trading restrictions against the importation of lightweight motorcycles, applied in certain European countries, Honda has opened production plants in Italy and Spain, the latter saving the famous Montesa marque from disappearing. In contrast, the surprising turn round in the fortunes of the Harley-Davidson Company in the USA has resulted in the trade embargo against Japan, imposed in 1983 on the importation of big bikes, being lifted this year. In Italy, the Cagiva group seems to have been successful in rationalizing the output of Ducati and Morini and another fast growing company there was Aprilia.

Technical change since the 1986 edition has been the search for yet more performance from compact, better-handling machines. The Kawasaki GPX600R with a 592 cc capacity engine delivers the equivalent of over 140 bhp per litre. Coupled to a light and streamlined frame speeds of over 225 km/h (140 mph) become possible. Such is the battle for sales between the Big Four from Japan that any comparisons of performance in the power race between Kawasaki's GPX600R, Honda's CBR600F, Suzuki's GSX600F and Yamaha's FZ600 will be academic for most riders and, in any case, certainly will be reversed at the next round of model updates.

Balancing power and handling is the secret of putting performance on the road and this is now being packaged in sleek, aerodynamically-tested full-enclosure fairings. Drag co-efficients have been quoted in the publicity for cars for several years, but now they are appearing in the sales jargon for motorcycles. Along with the slippery profile, there are engine management improvements to intake, combustion and exhaust efficiency, to ensure power delivery matches any demand at the throttle.

The requirement to get appearances right has resulted in some dramatic liberties being taken with the practice of body lining and badging on bikes. The once discrete tank badge has been overtaken by designer decals blazoned across the fresh expanses of bodywork that cover today's road racers.

Many of these technical enhancements are labelled on the bike in the form of cryptic acronyms, lest the rider forget. You will be told your bike is a V-Four, it is for Rally Touring, it has 5-valves, Twin Cams, Liquid Cooling. The engine runs better because it has YPVS, the Yamaha Power Valve System to provide variable exhaust timing, or SACS, Suzuki's Advanced Cooling System that uses oil for engine cooling and lubrication. The frame may be FAST, made by Featherweight Aluminium and Steel Technology and include a Full Floater Suspension with TRAC, Honda's Torque Reactive Anti-dive Control front fork. Stopping may be improved by BAC, Kawasaki's Balanced Actuation Caliper, and you might improve the comfort of the ride through ESCS, Kawasaki's Electric Suspension Control System, or adjustments to SPS, Suzuki's Power Shield, electric windscreen.

Turbo-charged bikes appeared in the last edition but that line of engine development seems, for the moment, to have been temporarily shelved. Anti-lock braking systems have moved even closer to production since the last edition and Honda is expected any day to market its variation of the Lucas-Girling hydro-mechanical unit. Although BMW was expected to be the first to introduce anti-lock braking on bikes, following a decade of successful use on its cars, none of the 1987 models featured in this edition have them as a standard fitting. The latest improvements in tyre technology have led to more bikes being fitted with fat profile radials, while the virtual disappearance of spoked wheels, except in lightweights or classic models, means that tubeless tyres are now very common fittings. The move towards smaller wheel sizes which brought in the 16-inch now seems to be reversing and many of the 1987 pace setters feature 17-inch wheels.

As with all previous editions, this book has been made possible by the helpful co-operation of manufacturers around the world and my thanks are extended for this assistance. While every effort has been made to ensure the book's accuracy it is not possible to guarantee all the specifications quoted as manufacturers always reserve the right to alter model details without notice. The motorcycles featured in this sixth edition are from the 1987 ranges and are in most cases built to United Kingdom or European market specifications.

Robert Croucher

Technical Specifications Explained

How to use this book

Model: Manufacturers identify each model in their bike range by a code made up of letters and numbers. Sometimes a model also gets a name. These codes describe the type of bike, its engine capacity and may indicate a special feature or the year of its introduction. The codes are not standardized and model labels such as SuperSport, GP or Special may mean different things to each manufacturer. Names are also being used to create an image for new engineering developments. Thus all Harley-Davidson models are now said to be running the 'Evolution' engine and the advanced design technology of Yamaha's FZ range is labelled 'Genesis'.

Engine: Motorcycle engines come in single or multi-cylinder form with a 2 or 4-stroke combustion cycle. 2-strokes are further classified by their fuel mixture intake system as piston port, reed or rotary disc valve. 4-stroke engines are described by their valve actuating mechanism as overhead valve (ohv), single (sohc), or double (dohc) overhead camshafts. Two valves per cylinder were customary for motorbike engines, but now the quest for better performance has led to four and even five valves being fitted (three inlet and two exhaust) to speed gas-flow rate and achieve improved combustion efficiency. Single cylinder engines normally sit vertically in the bike frame sloping slightly forward, but multi-cylinder configurations can be in-line across the frame, in a vee or flat formation to create twins, triples, fours and even sixes. The engines of sports bikes are now typically inclined forward at 45 degrees to improve weight distribution for better handling. LC indicates an engine with liquid cooling by water jacket and radiator. A new development is the use of oil cooling, but still most bike engines are air-cooled.

Capacity: The cubic content of the cylinder(s) measured in centimetres. This measure of engine size may be significant for taxation, insurance and safety legislation purposes. Bikes range in engine size from 49 cc tiddlers to mammoths of over 1 400 cc.

Bore × Stroke: An indication of the relationship between the cylinder head diameter and the length of the piston within it measured in millimetres. Modern motorcycle engines are often short stroke and square. Long stroke thumping is more characteristic of big touring bikes and the new, large capacity trail machines.

Compression ratio: A measure of the compression of the fuel/air mixture in each cylinder by the rising piston before ignition. A high compression engine would be one with a ratio of 9:1 or over.

Carburettor: This meters fuel and air to the engine. The number of carburettors, the choke size diameter and the make are given. The carburettor may be of the piston slide or constant velocity (cv) type.

Maximum power: The brake horsepower (bhp) and the engine speed (rpm) at which it is achieved are given. This figure can vary widely with the methods used to measure it. Most of the figures quoted in this book are to the German DIN standard which measures the net output of the engine under normal use conditions with pumps and generators working. *Starting:* Invariably now by push button electric starters. Some smaller bikes retain the kick-operated crank and mopeds may be started using pedals.

Transmission: The number of gears in the gearbox and the method of final drive to the rear wheel are given. Most bikes use a wet, multi-plate clutch to engage and disengage engine drive. Mopeds and scooters often use centrifugal clutches to give a completely automatic drive. Some machines are now fitted with belt drive rather than chains.

Electrics: A bike's electrical supply usually comes from a 12v battery. The ignition system is commonly electronic and maintenance-free. The battery capacity is described in ampere-hours (Ah). Some lightweight machines still use a 6v electrical supply with direct charging from a flywheel magneto. They may have a small dry cell battery to supply lighting when stationary.

Frame: Normally this is a strong tubular steel frame formed into a single or double cradle. Many high performance bikes feature square or box section frames in a diamond shape to combine strength with rigidity. Modern frames may be made of special steels (chrome-molybdenum) or to achieve lightness, aluminium. Some machines use pressed steel beams or spines with the engine suspended and acting as a stressed member. Scooters often have an integral monocoque body construction.

Suspension: The front suspension is usually by telescopic fork with compression and rebound damping by coil springs and hydraulic pressure. Some of the big bikes supplement this system with infinitely variable air pressure arrangements. Anti-dive systems have been developed on some models to further control the compression damping of the front fork under the load of severe braking. Conventionally, rear suspension is by swinging arm and hydraulic shock absorbers. For lightness, the swinging arm is often made from box section aluminium. The rear single shock system, designed originally for motocross racers, is now used on the majority of road machines because of its torsional rigidity and rising rate linkages. Monoshock systems come in various forms and the trade names include Honda's *Pro-Link*, Kawasaki's *Uni-Trak*, Suzuki's *Full-Floater* and Yamaha's *Monocross*. Uniquely, BMW's *Monoshock System* comprises a rigid single swinging arm with one offset shock absorber. Both the spring pre-load and the damping characteristics of rear shock absorbers may be adjustable to take account of extra load or particular road conditions.

Brakes: Braking can be drum or disc operated. The front hydraulic disc is now universal except on small bikes and scooters. Disc brake technology has developed lightweight drilled or slotted discs which prevent distortion under heavy use and dual-piston calipers (d-pc) to generate maximum braking force. Multi-piston design means that the friction pads can be located at the edge of the disc where the braking force is greatest while permitting the disc to be smaller and lighter. Sintered metal pad compounds mean that disc brakes are now much more efficient even in wet conditions. One interesting variation is the Moto Guzzi integral braking system which links front and rear discs through the foot pedal to provide balanced braking effort.

Tyres: Traditionally, motorcycle wheels are wire spoked but most bikes now feature cast aluminium, hollow-spoke wheels in a variety of styles. These reduce the bike's unsprung weight, improve suspension performance and permit the use of tubeless tyres. Front tyres are ribbed to give positive steering ability while the rear rubber is broader with a curved profile and deep zig-zag treads to grip the road on cornering and to transmit the power during acceleration. Tyre sizes are indicated in a variety of ways. A size of 3.50–18 indicates the tyre width and the wheelrim diameter in inches. But a tyre may also be described as 100/90V18 where the 100 measures the tyre width in millimetres, the 90 is a percentage and refers to the ratio between the height of the tyre and its width, and the 18 is the wheelrim diameter in inches. The letter V shows that the tyre is suitable for high speeds exceeding 200 km/h. Other markings are H for performance up to 200 km/h and S for standard road speeds. These speed ratings are based on correct inflation on the right rim size wheel, running within the designed load capacity. The 160/60V18 rear tyre on a Yamaha FZR1000 is an example of a wide-section, low-profile radial with ultra high-speed rating.

Dimensions: Metric measures are provided as illustrated in the following drawing of a BMW R80RT:

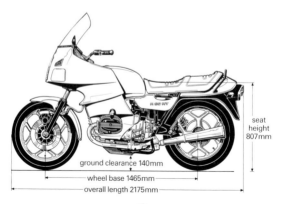

seat height 807mm

ground clearance 140mm

wheel base 1465mm

overall length 2175mm

The *Dry weight* figure provides a standard so that bikes can be compared regardless of any differences in fuel or oil capacity.

The *Fuel tank* figure is a maximum and usually includes 2 or 3 litres in reserve. In a pollution-conscious world, it is worth noting that most of the bikes available, whether 2 or 4-stroke, will happily run on lead-free petrol. Four-strokes will normally require 95 octane premium grade fuel.

Performance: Most manufacturers are reluctant to give performance figures for their motorcycles because what can be achieved clearly varies with the rider and the conditions under which the testing was carried out. The examples used in the book are averages of published test results or factory-approved figures and should be read as approximate limits rather than absolute benchmarks. Fuel consumption figures, in particular, can be very misleading when they are obtained under conditions of steady, slow-speed running. The figures given are based on the expected litres of fuel consumption over a distance of 100 kilometres and are only a rough guide to what might be obtained under typical, mixed riding conditions. 7 l/100 km is equivalent to 40 mpg.

Features: Details of any special equipment or alternative models.

Note
... This indicates that information is not available.

AGRATI-GARELLI (Italy)

Model: GTA 125

Engine: 2-str reed-valve LC single
Capacity: 124.8 cc
Bore × Stroke: 52.8 × 57 mm
Compression ratio: 14:1
Carburettor: 28 mm Dell'Orto
Maximum power: 22 bhp at 8 750 rpm
Starting: electric

Transmission: 6-speed chain

Electrics: 12 v electronic ignition with 9 Ah battery

Frame: Box section cradle

Suspension: Telehydraulic front fork with anti-dive and rear *Soft Lever* monoshock system.

Brakes: 240 mm triple drilled disc system with dual-piston calipers

Tyres: Front is 100/90–16
Rear is 100/90–18

Dimensions:
Length: 2 000 mm
Width: 570 mm
Wheelbase: 1 340 mm
Clearance: 140 mm
Seat height: 780 mm
Dry weight: 122 kg
Fuel tank: 18 litres

Performance:
Top speed: 135 km/h
Fuel consumption: 4.2 l/100 km

Features: Alloy wheels.

Manufacturer: Agrati-Garelli S.p.A., via Immacolata, 25, 22068 Monticello Brianza (Como), Italy.

AGRATI-GARELLI (Italy)

Model: Tiger 125 XRD

Engine: 2-str reed-valve LC
single
Capacity: 124.8 cc
Bore × Stroke: 52.8 × 57 mm
Compression ratio: 14:1
Carburettor: 28 mm Dell'Orto
Maximum power: 21 bhp at
8 250 rpm
Starting: electric

Transmission: 6-speed chain

Electrics: 12 v electronic
ignition with 5 Ah battery

Frame: Box section cradle

Suspension: Telehydraulic
front fork with rear *Soft Lever*
monoshock system.

Manufacturer: Agrati-Garelli S.p.A.

Brakes: 240 mm front disc and
220 mm rear disc

Tyres: Front is 3.00–21
Rear is 4.60–17

Dimensions:
Length: 2 140 mm
Width: 900 mm
Wheelbase: 1 370 mm
Clearance: ...
Seat height: 880 mm
Dry weight: 120 kg
Fuel tank: 18 litres

Performance:
Top speed: 126 km/h
Fuel consumption: 4.2 l/100 km

Features: Knuckle guards and
rear carrier. Also 50 cc model.

APRILIA (Italy)

Model: ETX 600

Engine: 4-str 4-valve LC single
Capacity: 561.83 cc
Bore × Stroke: 94 × 81 mm
Compression ratio: 9.6:1
Carburettor: 40 mm Dell'Orto
Maximum power: 49 bhp at
7 250 rpm
Starting: electric

Transmission: 5-speed chain

Electrics: 12 v electronic
ignition with 14 Ah battery

Frame: Duplex tubular cradle

Suspension: Telehydraulic
front fork with *Aprilia
Progressive* monoshock system
at the rear.

Brakes: 230 mm drilled disc
front and rear

Tyres: Front is 3.00–21
Rear is 5.10–17

Dimensions:
Length: 2 200 mm
Width: 860 mm
Wheelbase: 1 480 mm
Clearance: 300 mm
Seat height: 890 mm
Dry weight: 139 kg
Fuel tank: 14 litres

Performance:
Top speed: 160 km/h
Fuel consumption: 4.3 l/100 km

Features: Range includes
550 cc and 350 cc versions.

Manufacturer: Aprilia S.p.A., via G Galilei, 1, 30033 Noale (VE), Italy.

APRILIA (Italy)

Model: AS 125R

Engine: 2-str RAVE LC single
Capacity: 123.6 cc
Bore × Stroke: 54 × 54 mm
Compression ratio: 14.2:1
Carburettor: 28 mm Dell'Orto
Maximum power: 26 bhp at
8 500 rpm
Starting: kick

Transmission: 6-speed chain

Electrics: 12 v electronic
ignition

Frame: Duplex tubular cradle

Suspension: Telescopic front
fork with *APS* rear monoshock
system.

Manufacturer: Aprilia S.p.A.

Brakes: 240 mm drilled floating
disc and 230 mm rear disc

Tyres: Front is 100/90–16
Rear is 100/90–18

Dimensions:
Length: 2 015 mm
Width: 750 mm
Wheelbase: 1 365 mm
Clearance: 170 mm
Seat height: 800 mm
Dry weight: 107 kg
Fuel tank: 12 litres

Performance:
Top speed: 140 km/h
Fuel consumption: 4.5 l/100 km

Features: RAVE is Rotax
Automatic Variable Exhaust
valve control.

APRILIA (Italy)

Model: Tuareg 50

Engine: 2-str Rotax LC single
Capacity: 49.6 cc
Bore × Stroke: 38.8 × 42 mm
Compression ratio: 11:1
Carburettor: 12 mm Dell'Orto
Maximum power: 1.5 bhp at
3 750 rpm
Starting: kick

Transmission: 4-speed chain

Electrics: 12 v electronic
ignition

Frame: Split single beam

Suspension: Telescopic front
fork with *APS* rear monoshock
system.

Manufacturer: Aprilia S.p.A.

Brakes: 230 mm front disc and
118 mm rear drum

Tyres: Front is 2.75–21
Rear is 3.50–18

Dimensions:
Length: 2 070 mm
Width: 805 mm
Wheelbase: 1 330 mm
Clearance: . . .
Seat height: 845 mm
Dry weight: 80 kg
Fuel tank: 18 litres

Performance:
Top speed: 40 km/h
Fuel consumption: 2 l/100 km

Features: Also as 125 cc and
250 cc models.

BENELLI (Italy)

Model: 900 Sei

Engine: 4-str sohc in-line six
Capacity: 905.9 cc
Bore × Stroke: 60 × 53.4 mm
Compression ratio: 9.5:1
Carburettor: 3 × 24 mm Dell'Orto
Maximum power: 80 bhp at
8 400 rpm
Starting: electric

Transmission: 5-speed chain

Electrics: 12 v electronic
ignition with 28 Ah battery

Frame: Duplex tubular cradle

Suspension: Telescopic front
fork with twin adjustable rear
dampers.

Brakes: 300 mm twin discs and
260 mm rear disc

Tyres: Front is 100/90V18
Rear is 120/90V18

Dimensions:
Length: 2 110 mm
Width: 690 mm
Wheelbase: 1 460 mm
Clearance: 150 mm
Seat height: 790 mm
Dry weight: 220 kg
Fuel tank: 16.5 litres

Performance:
Top speed: 215 km/h
Fuel consumption: 8 l/100 km

Features: Linked braking
system 3-into-2 exhaust
arrangement. Modern six
cylinder classic.

Manufacturer: F.lli Benelli S.p.A., Chiusa di Ginestreto, 61100, Pesaro,
Italy.

BENELLI (Italy)

Model: 125 BX

Engine: 2-str LC single
Capacity: 123.15 cc
Bore × Stroke: 56 × 50 mm
Compression ratio: 7:1
Carburettor: 24 mm Dell'Orto
Maximum power: 20 bhp at
8 000 rpm
Starting: kick

Transmission: 6-speed chain

Electrics: 12 v electronic
ignition with 7 Ah battery

Frame: Box section cradle

Suspension: Marzocchi air fork
with rear hydraulic monoshock.

Manufacturer: F.lli. Benelli S.p.A.

Brakes: 260 mm shrouded
front disc and 125 mm drum

Tyres: Front is 2.75–21
Rear is 4.10–18

Dimensions:
Length: 1 860 mm
Width: 715 mm
Wheelbase: 1 220 mm
Clearance: . . .
Seat height: . . .
Dry weight: 105 kg
Fuel tank: 10 litres

Performance:
Top speed: 115 km/h
Fuel consumption: 3.3 l/100 km

Features: Optional electric
start. Rear carrier.

BETA (Italy)

Model: KR 250

Engine: 2-str reed-valve LC single
Capacity: 239 cc
Bore × Stroke: 72.8 × 57.5 mm
Compression ratio: 11.5:1
Carburettor: 25 mm Dell'Orto
Maximum power: 22 bhp at 5 200 rpm
Starting: kick

Transmission: 5-speed chain

Electrics: 12 v electronic ignition

Frame: Box section steel cradle

Suspension: Marzocchi gas fork with adjustable monoshock system.

Brakes: 230 mm shrouded front disc and 140 mm rear drum

Tyres: Front is 3.00–21
Rear is 4.00–18

Dimensions:
Length: ...
Width: ...
Wheelbase: 1 370 mm
Clearance: ...
Seat height: 845 mm
Dry weight: 104 kg
Fuel tank: 10 litres

Performance:
Top speed: 140 km/h
Fuel consumption: ...

Features: High level exhaust knuckle guards, rear carrier. Also in 125 cc version. Afrika version has large 20 litre tank.

Manufacturer: Betamotor S.p.A., via Roma, 50067 Rignano sull'arno (FI), Italy.

BETA (Italy)

Model: Trekking

Engine: 2-str reed valve single
Capacity: 239.2 cc
Bore × Stroke: 72.8 × 57.5 mm
Compression ratio: 11:1
Carburettor: 26 mm Dell'Orto
Maximum power: 13 bhp at
5 000 rpm
Starting: kick

Transmission: 6-speed chain

Electrics: 12 v electronic
ignition

Frame: Tubular cradle

Suspension: Telescopic front
fork with rear adjustable
monoshock.

Manufacturer: Betamotor S.p.A.

Brakes: 125 mm drums front
and rear

Tyres: Front is 2.75–21
Rear is 4.00–18

Dimensions:
Length: 2 020
Width: ...
Wheelbase: 1 310 mm
Clearance: 350 mm
Seat height: 850 mm
Dry weight: 92 kg
Fuel tank: 5 litres

Performance:
Top speed: 96 km/h
Fuel consumption: ...

Features: Dual purpose bike.

BIMOTA (Italy)

Model: yb5

Engine: 4-str dohc Yamaha parallel four
Capacity: 1 188 cc
Bore × Stroke: 77 × 63.8 mm
Compression ratio: 9.7:1
Carburettor: 4 × 36 mm Mikuni
Maximum power: 130.5 bhp at 8 700 rpm
Starting: electric

Transmission: 5-speed chain

Electrics: 12 v electronic ignition with 14 Ah battery

Frame: Chrom-moly steel space type

Suspension: Telehydraulic front fork with anti-dive and rear adjustable monoshock system.

Brakes: 300 mm twin floating discs and single 260 mm rear disc

Tyres: Front is 120/60VR18
Rear is 160/60VR18

Dimensions:
Length: 2 100 mm
Width: 680 mm
Wheelbase: 1 455 mm
Clearance: 170 mm
Seat height: 800 mm
Dry weight: 216kg
Fuel tank: 22 litres

Performance:
Top speed: 260 km/h
Fuel consumption: 6.6 l/100 km

Features: Radial, tubeless tyres. Streamlined body casing, steering damper.

Manufacturer: Bimota S.p.A., via Giaccaglia, 38, 47037 Rimini, Italy.

BIMOTA (Italy)

Model: db1 SR

Engine: 4-str sohc 90° vee-twin
Capacity: 748 cc
Bore × Stroke: 88 × 61.5 mm
Compression ratio: 10.4:1
Carburettor: 2 × 36 mm Dell'Orto
Maximum power: 70 bhp at
8 500 rpm
Starting: electric

Transmission: 5-speed chain

Electrics: 12 v electronic
ignition with 14 Ah battery

Frame: Chrome-moly steel in a
trestle shape

Suspension: Telescopic front
fork with anti-dive and single rear
adjustable central damper.

Manufacturer: Bimota S.p.A.

Brakes: 280 mm twin floating
disc with rear 220 mm disc

Tyres: Front is 130/60VR16
Rear is 160/60VR16

Dimensions:
Length: 2 000 mm
Width: 630 mm
Wheelbase: 1 380 mm
Clearance: 160 mm
Seat height: 800 mm
Dry weight: 160 kg
Fuel tank: 21 litres

Performance:
Top speed: 210 km/h
Fuel consumption: 4.6 l/100 km

Features: Fitted with radial
tyres.

BMW (West Germany)

Model: K100LT

Engine: 4-str dohc LC in-line flat four
Capacity: 987 cc
Bore × Stroke: 67 × 70 mm
Compression ratio: 10.2:1
Carburettor: injection
Maximum power: 90 bhp at 8 000 rpm
Starting: electric

Transmission: 5-speed shaft drive

Electrics: 12 v digital ignition with 20 Ah battery

Frame: Tubular space with engine as a loadbearing component

Suspension: Telescopic front fork with rear *Monolever* system.

Brakes: 285 mm triple slotted disc system

Tyres: Front is 100/90V18
Rear is 130/90V17

Dimensions:
Length: 2 220 mm
Width: 916 mm
Wheelbase: 1 516 mm
Clearance: 175 mm
Seat height: 810 mm
Dry weight: 239 kg
Fuel tank: 22 litres

Performance:
Top speed: 215 km/h
Fuel consumption: 5.4 l/100 km

Features: Aerodynamic touring fairing, high handlebar, clock, integral touring cases. Options include heated grips, radio and self-levelling suspension.

Manufacturer: BMW Motorrad AG, 8000 München 45, West Germany.

23

BMW (West Germany)

Model: R100RS

Engine: 4-str ohv horizontally-opposed twin
Capacity: 980 cc
Bore × Stroke: 94 × 70.6 mm
Compression ratio: 8.45:1
Carburettor: 2 × 32 mm Bing
Maximum power: 60 bhp at 6 500 rpm
Starting: electric

Transmission: 5-speed shaft drive

Electrics: 12 v electronic ignition with 30 Ah battery

Frame: Duplex tubular cradle

Suspension: Telescopic front fork with rear *Monolever* system.

Manufacturer: BMW Motorrad AG

Brakes: Twin 285 mm slotted front discs and 200 mm rear drum

Tyres: 90/90H18 front and rear

Dimensions:
Length: 2 175 mm
Width: 800 mm
Wheelbase: 1 447 mm
Clearance: 125 mm
Seat height: 807 mm
Dry weight: 207 kg
Fuel tank: 22 litres

Performance:
Top speed: 185 km/h
Fuel consumption: 6.1 l/100 km

Features: Oil cooler, sports fairing, rear carrier. Re-launched classic model first available in 1976. Y-design alloy wheels.

BMW (West Germany)

Model: R80RT

Engine: 4-str ohv horizontally-opposed twin
Capacity: 798 cc
Bore × Stroke: 84 × 70.6 mm
Compression ratio: 8.2:1
Carburettor: 2 × 32 mm Bing
Maximum power: 50 bhp at 6 500 rpm
Starting: electric

Transmission: 5-speed shaft drive

Electrics: 12 v electronic ignition with 20 Ah battery

Frame: Duplex tubular cradle

Suspension: Telescopic front fork with rear *Monolever* system.

Manufacturer: BMW Motorrad AG.

Brakes: 285 mm front disc with 200 mm rear drum

Tyres: Front is 90/90H18
Rear is 120/90H18

Dimensions:
Length: 2 175 mm
Width: 960 mm
Wheelbase: 1 465 mm
Clearance: 140 mm
Seat height: 807 mm
Dry weight: 205 kg
Fuel tank: 22 litres

Performance:
Top speed: 170 km/h
Fuel consumption: 7.2 l/100km

Features: Fully equipped tourer adjustable windscreen, luggage panniers, high-rise handlebars.

BMW (West Germany)

Model: R80G/S

Engine: 4-str ohv horizontally-opposed twin
Capacity: 798 cc
Bore × Stroke: 84 × 70.6 mm
Compression ratio: 8.2:1
Carburettor: 2 × 32 mm Bing
Maximum power: 50 bhp at 6 500 rpm
Starting: electric

Transmission: 5-speed shaft drive

Electrics: 12 v electronic ignition with 20 Ah battery

Frame: Duplex tubular cradle

Suspension: Telescopic front fork with rear *Monolever* system and new Paralever, double-joint swinging arm to reduce shaft load reactions.

Manufacturer: BMW Motorrad AG.

Brakes: 260 mm front disc and 200 mm rear drum

Tyres: Front is 3.00–21
Rear is 4.00–18

Dimensions:
Length: 2 230 mm
Width: 746 mm
Wheelbase: 1 485 mm
Clearance: 200 mm
Seat height: 860 mm
Dry weight: 170 kg
Fuel tank: 19.5 litres

Performance:
Top speed: 168 km/h
Fuel consumption: 5.5 l/100 km

Features: Dual purpose bike. Also available in Paris-Dakar styling. 1988 range includes 60 bhp one litre version.

BMW (West Germany)

Model: K75S

Engine: 4-str dohc LC flat triple
Capacity: 740 cc
Bore × Stroke: 67 × 70 mm
Compression ratio: 11:1
Carburettor: injection
Maximum power: 75 bhp at
8 500 rpm
Starting: electric

Transmission: 5-speed shaft
drive

Electrics: 12 v digital ignition
with 20 Ah battery

Frame: Tubular space with
engine as a loadbearing
component

Suspension: Telescopic front
fork with rear *Monolever* system.

Manufacturer: BMW Motorrad AG

Brakes: 285 mm triple slotted
disc system

Tyres: Front is 100/90V18
Rear is 130/90V17

Dimensions:
Length: 2 220 mm
Width: 810 mm
Wheelbase: 1 510 mm
Clearance: 175 mm
Seat height: 810 mm
Dry weight: 214 kg
Fuel tank: 21 litres

Performance:
Top speed: 210 km/h
Fuel consumption: 5 l/100 km

Features: Compact Drive
System. Bosch LE-Jetronic fuel
injection. Digital clock and
frame-fitted fairing. Optional
engine spoiler. Special paintwork
in black or silver.

BMW (West Germany)

Model: K75

Engine: 4-str dohc LC flat triple
Capacity: 740 cc
Bore × Stroke: 67 × 70 mm
Compression ratio: 11:1
Carburettor: injection
Maximum power: 75 bhp at
8 500 rpm
Starting: electric

Transmission: 5-speed shaft
drive

Electrics: 12 v digital ignition
with 20 Ah battery

Frame: Tubular space with
engine as a loadbearing
component

Suspension: Telescopic front
fork with rear *Monolever* system.

Manufacturer: BMW Motorrad AG.

Brakes: twin 285 mm discs and
rear 200 mm drum

Tyres: Front is 100/90H18
Rear is 120/90H18

Dimensions:
Length: 2 220 mm
Width: 900 mm
Wheelbase: 1 510 mm
Clearance: 175 mm
Seat height: 760 (810) mm
Dry weight: 207 kg
Fuel tank: 21 litres

Performance:
Top speed: 200 km/h
Fuel consumption: 5.2 l/100 km

Features: Compact Drive
System, Bosch LE-Jetronic fuel
injection. Luggage rack. K75C
has cockpit fairing.

BMW (West Germany)

Model: R65

Engine: 4-str ohv horizontally-opposed twin
Capacity: 650 cc
Bore × Stroke: 82 × 61.5 mm
Compression ratio: 8.7:1
Carburettor: 2 × 32 mm Bing
Maximum power: 48 bhp at 7 250 rpm
Starting: electric

Transmission: 5-speed shaft drive

Electrics: 12 v electronic ignition with 20 Ah battery

Frame: Duplex tubular cradle

Suspension: Telescopic front fork with rear *Monolever* system.

Manufacturer: BMW Motorrad AG

Brakes: 285 mm front disc with 200 mm rear drum

Tyres: Front is 90/90H18
Rear is 120/90H18

Dimensions:
Length: 2 175 mm
Width: 800 mm
Wheelbase: 1 465 mm
Clearance: 140 mm
Seat height: 807 mm
Dry weight: 185 kg
Fuel tank: 22 litres

Performance:
Top speed: 173 km/h
Fuel consumption: 6.4 l/100 km

Features: Similar to R80 model.

BOMBARDIER CAN-AM (Canada)

Model: 500 ASE

Engine: 2-str rotary valve single
Capacity: 482.3 cc
Bore × Stroke: 85 × 85 mm
Compression ratio: ...
Carburettor: 38 mm Mikuni
Maximum power: 50 bhp
Starting: kick

Transmission: 5-speed chain

Electrics: Bosch CDI ignition

Frame: Reynolds 531 tubular cradle

Suspension: Marzocchi M1 forks and adjustable *White Power* piggyback monoshock system.

Brakes: 240 mm front disc and 140 mm rear drum

Tyres: Front is 3.00–21
Rear is 180/90–18

Dimensions:
Length: ...
Width: ...
Wheelbase: 1 511 mm
Clearance: 353 mm
Seat height: 965 mm
Dry weight: 111.5 kg
Fuel tank: 12 litres

Performance:
Top speed: ...
Fuel consumption: ...

Features: Quick-detach rear wheel with snail-cam chain adjusters. Enduro lighting, Rotax engine. The range includes 200, 250 and 406 models.

Manufacturer: Bombardier Inc, Valcourt, Quebec, Canada JOE 2L0.

BSA (England)

Model: 125/6 Tracker

Engine: 2-str reed-valve single
Capacity: 123 cc
Bore × Stroke: 56 × 50 mm
Compression ratio: 7.2:1
Carburettor: 22 mm Mikuni
Maximum power: 12 bhp at
7 000 rpm
Starting: kick

Transmission: 6-speed chain

Electrics: 6 v flywheel magneto
with 4 Ah battery

Frame: Tubular cradle

Suspension: Telescopic front
fork with rear single monoshock
system.

Brakes: 160 mm front drum
and 140 mm rear drum

Tyres: Front is 2.75–21
Rear is 3.50–18

Dimensions:
Length: 2 000 mm
Width: 899 mm
Wheelbase: 1 320 mm
Clearance: 240 mm
Seat height: 750 mm
Dry weight: 94 kg
Fuel tank: 4.6 litres

Performance:
Top speed: 110 km/h
Fuel consumption: 3 l/100 km

Features: Assembled in UK
from imported components. Also
in 175 cc version.

Manufacturer: BSA Co. Ltd, Units 98 & 99 Northwick Park Business
Centre, Blockley, Nr Moreton in Marsh, Gloucestershire GL56 9RF,
England.

CAGIVA (Italy)

Model: 750 Lucky Explorer

Engine: 4-str Desmo 90° twin
Capacity: 748 cc
Bore × Stroke: 88 × 61.5 mm
Compression ratio: 10:1
Carburettor: 2 × 32 mm Bing
Maximum power: 60.5 bhp at
8 000 rpm
Starting: electric and kick

Transmission: 5-speed chain

Electrics: 12 v electronic
ignition

Frame: Box section cradle

Suspension: Telehydraulic
front fork with *Soft Damp* single
rear shocker.

Brakes: 260 mm drilled floating
disc and 240 mm rear disc

Tyres: Front is 90/90–21
Rear is 130/80–17

Dimensions:
Length: 2 290 mm
Width: 885 mm
Wheelbase: 1 520 mm
Clearance: 240 mm
Seat height: 905 mm
Dry weight: 184 kg
Fuel tank: 19 litres

Performance:
Top speed: 200 km/h
Fuel consumption: 6.5 l/100 km

Features: Paris-Dakar Rally
model. Plastic disc and fork
protectors.

Manufacturer: Cagiva S.p.A., via A Cavalieri, 3, 40132 Bologna, Italy.

CAGIVA (Italy)

Model: T4 500E

Engine: 4-str sohc 4-valve
single
Capacity: 452 cc
Bore × Stroke: 94 × 65 mm
Compression ratio: 9:1
Carburettor: 40 mm Bing
Maximum power: 40 bhp at
7 000 rpm
Starting: electric

Transmission: 5-speed chain

Electrics: 12 v electronic
ignition

Frame: Duplex tubular cradle

Suspension: Telehydraulic
front fork with *Soft Damp* single
rear shocker.

Manufacturer: Cagiva S.p.A.

Brakes: 240 mm drilled front
disc and rear 130 mm drum

Tyres: Front is 3.00–21
Rear is 5.10–17

Dimensions:
Length: 2 160 mm
Width: 860 mm
Wheelbase: 1 460 mm
Clearance: 300 mm
Seat height: 900 mm
Dry weight: 140 kg
Fuel tank: 12 litres

Performance:
Top speed: 155 km/h
Fuel consumption: ...

Features: Plastic disc brake
protector. Range includes 350E
and 350R versions.

CAGIVA (Italy)

Model: 350 Elefant Big Belly

Engine: 4-str sohc Pantah 90°
vee-twin
Capacity: 349 cc
Bore × Stroke: 66 × 51 mm
Compression ratio: 10.3:1
Carburettor: 2 × 32 mm Bing
Maximum power: 36.5 bhp at
8 000 rpm
Starting: electric and kick

Transmission: 5-speed chain

Electrics: 12 v electronic
ignition

Frame: Box section cradle

Suspension: Telehydraulic
front fork with *Soft Damp* single
rear shocker.

Manufacturer: Cagiva S.p.A.

Brakes: 260 mm drilled floating
disc and 240 mm rear disc

Tyres: Front is 3.00–21
Rear is 5.10–17

Dimensions:
Length: 2 290 mm
Width: 885 mm
Wheelbase: 1 520 mm
Clearance: 240 mm
Seat height: 905 mm
Dry weight: 178 kg
Fuel tank: 30 litres

Performance:
Top speed: 150 km/h
Fuel consumption: 5 l/100 km

Features: Elefant range
includes a 125, 200 and 650
version.

CAGIVA (Italy)

Model: Alazzurra 350

Engine: 4-str sohc 90° Desmo
vee-twin
Capacity: 349 cc
Bore × Stroke: 66 × 51 mm
Compression ratio: 10.3:1
Carburettor: 2 × 28 mm Dell'Orto
Maximum power: 34 bhp at
10 000 rpm
Starting: electric

Transmission: 5-speed chain

Electrics: 12 v electronic
ignition with 20 Ah battery

Frame: Tubular bridge type

Suspension: Telehydraulic
front fork with *Koni* adjustable
rear dampers.

Manufacturer: Cagiva S.p.A.

Brakes: 260 mm triple drilled
floating disc system

Tyres: Front is 90/90H18
Rear is 110/80H18

Dimensions:
Length: 2 160 mm
Width: 710 mm
Wheelbase: 1 460 mm
Clearance: 175 mm
Seat height: 800 mm
Dry weight: 182 kg
Fuel tank: 18 litres

Performance:
Top speed: 160 km/h
Fuel consumption: 5.2 l/100 km

Features: Also as 650 cc
model.

CAGIVA (Italy)

Model: Freccia 125

Engine: 2-str reed-valve LC single
Capacity: 124.6 cc
Bore × Stroke: 56 × 50.6 mm
Compression ratio: 13:1
Carburettor: 28 mm Dell'Orto
Maximum power: 27 bhp at 10 000 rpm
Starting: electric

Transmission: 6-speed chain

Electrics: 12 v electronic ignition

Frame: Box section cradle

Suspension: Telehydraulic front fork with anti-dive and *Soft Damp* variable single shock system at the rear.

Manufacturer: Cagiva S.p.A.

Brakes: 260 mm drilled floating disc and 240 mm rear disc

Tyres: Front is 100/80–16
Rear is 110/80–16

Dimensions:
Length: 1 960 mm
Width: 625 mm
Wheelbase: 1 370 mm
Clearance: 170 mm
Seat height: 770 mm
Dry weight: 123 kg
Fuel tank: 16 litres

Performance:
Top speed: over 150 km/h
Fuel consumption: ...

Features: Aerodynamic styling. Controlled Air Flow scoop for front fender.

CAGIVA (Italy)

Model: Cruiser 125

Engine: 2-str reed-valve LC single
Capacity: 124.6 cc
Bore × Stroke: 56 × 50.6 mm
Compression ratio: 13:1
Carburettor: 28 mm Dell'Orto
Maximum power: 27 bhp at 9 000 rpm
Starting: electric and kick

Transmission: 6-speed chain

Electrics: 12 v electronic ignition

Frame: Box section cradle

Suspension: Telehydraulic front fork with *Soft Damp* single rear shocker.

Manufacturer: Cagiva S.p.A.

Brakes: 230 mm drilled floating disc and 220 mm rear disc

Tyres: Front is 2.75–21
Rear is 4.60–17

Dimensions:
Length: 2 110 mm
Width: 820 mm
Wheelbase: 1 394 mm
Clearance: 305 mm
Seat height: 890 mm
Dry weight: 120 kg
Fuel tank: 14 litres

Performance:
Top speed: ...
Fuel consumption: ...

Features: Powerful enduro bike. Power jet carburettor, twin radiators, plastic shrouding on brakes and front fork.

CAGIVA (Italy)

Model: Aletta Oro 125

Engine: 2-str reed-valve LC single
Capacity: 124.6 cc
Bore × Stroke: 56 × 50.6 mm
Compression ratio: 11:1
Carburettor: 28 mm Dell'Orto
Maximum power: 21 bhp at 9 000 rpm
Starting: electric start

Transmission: 6-speed chain

Electrics: 12 v electronic ignition with 12 Ah battery

Frame: Box section cradle

Suspension: Telehydraulic front fork and *Soft Damp* variable single shock system at the rear.

Manufacturer: Cagiva S.p.A.

Brakes: 220 mm drilled floating discs front and rear

Tyres: Front is 90/100S16
Rear is 100/90S18

Dimensions:
Length: 2 050 mm
Width: 695 mm
Wheelbase: 1 380 mm
Clearance: 160 mm
Seat height: 787 mm
Dry weight: 124 kg
Fuel tank: 22 litres

Performance:
Top speed: 140 km/h
Fuel consumption: 5 l/100 km

Features: Racing styled fairing with bean can exhaust. LED fuel gauge.

CAGIVA (Italy)

Model: Aletta 125 Classic

Engine: 2-str reed-valve single
Capacity: 123.15 cc
Bore × Stroke: 56 × 50 mm
Compression ratio: 11.7:1
Carburettor: 24 mm Dell'Orto
Maximum power: 13.5 bhp at
7 250 rpm
Starting: electric and kick

Transmission: 6-speed chain

Electrics: 12 v electronic
ignition with 12 Ah battery

Frame: Duplex tubular cradle

Suspension: Telehydraulic
front fork with *Soft Damp* single
rear shocker.

Manufacturer: Cagiva S.p.A.

Brakes: Front disc and rear
drum

Tyres: Front is 3.00–18
Rear is 3.50–18

Dimensions:
Length: 2 050 mm
Width: 780 mm
Wheelbase: 1 360 mm
Clearance: 210 mm
Seat height: 810 mm
Dry weight: 112 kg
Fuel tank: 10.5 litres

Performance:
Top speed: 120 km/h
Fuel consumption: 4 l/100 km

Features: Cockpit fairing, cast
alloy wheels. Rear carrier.

CASAL (Portugal)

Model: K276

Engine: 2-str piston port single
Capacity: 123.7 cc
Bore × Stroke: 54 × 54 mm
Compression ratio: 10:1
Carburettor: 26 mm Bing
Maximum power: 14 bhp at
6 500 rpm
Starting: kick

Transmission: 6-speed chain

Electrics: 12 v electronic
ignition

Frame: Duplex tubular cradle

Suspension: Telescopic front
fork with twin rear hydraulic
dampers.

Brakes: 140 mm front drum
and 160 mm rear drum

Tyres: Front is 2.75–21
Rear is 3.50–18

Dimensions:
Length: 2 020 mm
Width: 830 mm
Wheelbase: 1 330 mm
Clearance: 170 mm
Seat height: 830 mm
Dry weight: 107 kg
Fuel tank: 9 litres

Performance:
Top speed: 120 km/h
Fuel consumption: 4.5 l/100 km

Features: Range includes
K551 and K506 trail model.

Manufacturer: Metalurgia Casal S.A.R.L., Apartado 83, 3801 Aveiro,
Portugal.

CZ (Czechoslovakia)

Model: CZ350

Engine: 2-str piston port single
Capacity: 343.47 cc
Bore × Stroke: 58 × 65 mm
Compression ratio: 9.5:1
Carburettor: 26 mm Jikov
Maximum power: 22 bhp at
5 000 rpm
Starting: kick

Transmission: 4-speed chain

Electrics: 12 v coil ignition with
5 Ah battery

Frame: Tubular cradle

Suspension: Telescopic front
fork with twin rear adjustable
dampers.

Brakes: 160 mm drums front
and rear

Tyres: Front is 3.25–18M10
Rear is 3.50–18M9

Dimensions:
Length: 2 010 mm
Width: 770 mm
Wheelbase: 1 320 mm
Clearance: 110 mm
Seat height: 820 mm
Dry weight: 170 kg
Fuel tank: 18 litres

Performance:
Top speed: 125 km/h
Fuel consumption: 4.6 l/100 km

Features: Range includes type
487 175 cc model.

Manufacturer: České Zàvody Motocyklové Strakonice,
Czechoslovakia.

CZ (Czechoslovakia)

Model: CZ125

Engine: 2-str single
Capacity: 123.2 cc
Bore × Stroke: 52 × 58 mm
Compression ratio: 8.6:1
Carburettor: 24 mm Jikov
Maximum power: 11 bhp at
5 500 rpm
Starting: kick

Transmission: 4-speed chain

Electrics: 6 v coil ignition with
5 Ah battery

Frame: Tubular cradle

Suspension: Telescopic front
fork with twin adjustable rear
dampers.

Manufacturer: CZM Strakonice.

Brakes: 160 mm drums front
and rear

Tyres: Front is 2.75–18
Rear is 3.00–18

Dimensions:
Length: 2 010 mm
Width: 715 mm
Wheelbase: 1 320 mm
Clearance: 125 mm
Seat height: 800 mm
Dry weight: 129 kg
Fuel tank: 13 litres

Performance:
Top speed: 90 km/h
Fuel consumption: 3.4 l/100 km

Features: Petroil lubrication
cockpit fairing available.

DERBI (Spain)

Model: Variant Sport 50

Engine: 2-str single
Capacity: 49.939 cc
Bore × Stroke: 39.87 × 40 mm
Compression ratio: 10:1
Carburettor: 12 mm Dell'Orto
Maximum power: 2 bhp at
5 500 rpm
Starting: pedal

Transmission: Single speed
automatic

Electrics: 6 v Motoplat ignition

Frame: Pressed steel step-thru

Suspension: Telescopic front
fork with twin rear dampers.

Brakes: 105 mm drums front
and rear

Tyres: 2.50–17 front and rear

Dimensions:
Length: 1 780 mm
Width: 690 mm
Wheelbase: 1 200 mm
Clearance: 140 mm
Seat height: 770 mm
Dry weight: 55 kg
Fuel tank: 3.3 litres

Performance:
Top speed: ...
Fuel consumption: ...

Features: Cast alloy wheels,
fully enclosed chain. Five
variants of this model available.

Manufacturer: Derbi Nacional Motor, S.A., 08100 Martorelles,
Barcelona, Spain.

DERBI (Spain)

Model: FDS

Engine: 2-str single
Capacity: 48.767 cc
Bore × Stroke: 38 × 43 mm
Compression ratio: 10.5:1
Carburettor: 12 mm Dell'Orto
Maximum power: 2 bhp at
8 000 rpm
Starting: kick

Transmission: 4-speed chain

Electrics: 6 v Motoplat ignition

Frame: Duplex tubular cradle

Suspension: Telehydraulic
front fork with *Derbi Track*
monoshock system.

Brakes: Covered 220 mm front
disc and 105 mm rear drum

Tyres: Front is 2.25–21
Rear is 2.25–18

Dimensions:
Length: 1 985 mm
Width: 830 mm
Wheelbase: 1 300 mm
Clearance: 310 mm
Seat height: 895 mm
Dry weight: . . .
Fuel tank: 7 litres

Performance:
Top speed: . . .
Fuel consumption: . . .

Features:

Manufacturer: Derbi Nacional Motor S.A.

DERBI (Spain)

Model: FD

Engine: 2-str single
Capacity: 48.767 cc
Bore × Stroke: 38 × 43 mm
Compression ratio: 10.5:1
Carburettor: 12 mm Dell'Orto
Maximum power: 2 bhp at
8 000 rpm
Starting: kick

Transmission: 4-speed chain

Electrics: 6 v Motoplat ignition

Frame: Duplex tubular cradle

Suspension: Telehydraulic
front fork with twin rear dampers.

Brakes: 220 mm front disc and
130 mm rear drum

Tyres: Front is 2.25–21
Rear is 3.25–18

Dimensions:
Length: 1 955 mm
Width: 800 mm
Wheelbase: 1 300 mm
Clearance: 310 mm
Seat height: 885 mm
Dry weight: ...
Fuel tank: 7.25 litres

Performance:
Top speed: ...
Fuel consumption: ...

Features: High level exhaust.

Manufacturer: Derbi Nacional Motor, S.A.

DERBI (Spain)

Model: Coppa FDT50

Engine: 2-str single
Capacity: 48.767 cc
Bore × Stroke: 38 × 43 mm
Compression ratio: 10.5:1
Carburettor: 12 mm Dell'Orto
Maximum power: 2 bhp at
8 000 rpm
Starting: kick

Transmission: 4-speed chain

Electrics: 6 v Motoplat ignition

Frame: Duplex tubular cradle

Suspension: Telehydraulic
front fork and single rear
monoshock system.

Brakes: 220 mm front disc
with 105 mm rear drum

Tyres: 2.50–17 front and rear

Dimensions:
Length: 1 960 mm
Width: 650 mm
Wheelbase: 1 295 mm
Clearance: 185 mm
Seat height: 750 mm
Dry weight: 55 kg
Fuel tank: 5 litres

Performance:
Top speed: . . .
Fuel consumption: . . .

Features: Handlebar fairing
and fashionable belly pan, cast
alloy wheels.

Manufacturer: Derbi Nacional Motor, S.A.

DERBI (Spain)

Model: Start DS-50

Engine: 2-str single
Capacity: 49.9 cc
Bore × Stroke: 39.87 × 40 mm
Compression ratio: 10:1
Carburettor: 12 mm Dell'Orto
Maximum power: 2 bhp at
6 400 rpm
Starting: kick

Transmission: single speed
automatic

Electrics: 6 v Motoplat ignition

Frame: Monocoque

Suspension: Telescopic front
fork with twin rear dampers.

Brakes: 105 mm drums front
and rear

Tyres: 3.00–10 front and rear

Dimensions:
Length: 1 715 mm
Width: 670 mm
Wheelbase: 1 180 mm
Clearance: 100 mm
Seat height: 795 mm
Dry weight: . . .
Fuel tank: 4.2 litres

Performance:
Top speed: . . .
Fuel consumption: . . .

Features:

Manufacturer: Derbi Nacional Motor, S.A.

DUCATI (Italy)

Model: 750 F1

Engine: 4-str Desmo valve 90° vee-twin
Capacity: 748 cc
Bore × Stroke: 88 × 61.5 mm
Compression ratio: 10:1
Carburettor: 2 × 36 mm Dell'Orto
Maximum power: 76 bhp at 9 000 rpm
Starting: electric

Transmission: 5-speed chain

Electrics: 12 v electronic ignition with 14 Ah battery

Frame: Tubular chrome-moly lattice bridge type

Suspension: Telehydraulic front fork with anti-dive and rear adjustable monoshock system.

Brakes: 280 mm dual drilled floating discs and rear 260 mm disc

Tyres: Front is 120/80V16
Rear is 130/80V18

Dimensions:
Length: 2 050 mm
Width: 670 mm
Wheelbase: 1 400 mm
Clearance: 165 mm
Seat height: 780 mm
Dry weight: 165 kg
Fuel tank: 18 litres

Performance:
Top speed: 220 km/h
Fuel consumption: 6.6 l/100 km

Features: Pantah engine. F3 is a 350 cc version. Steering damper.

Manufacturer: Cagiva-Ducati S.p.A., via A Cavalieri Ducati, 3, Bologna, Italy.

DUCATI (Italy)

Model: Paso 750

Engine: 4-str Desmo valve 90°
vee-twin
Capacity: 748 cc
Bore × Stroke: 88 × 61.5 mm
Compression ratio: 10:1
Carburettor: 2 × 44 mm Weber
Maximum power: 74 bhp at
7 900 rpm
Starting: electric

Transmission: 5-speed chain

Electrics: 12 v electronic
ignition with 14 Ah battery

Frame: Box section cradle

Suspension: Telehydraulic
front fork with anti-dive and rear
adjustable *Ohlins* single shock
system.

Brakes: 280 mm dual drilled
floating discs and rear 270 mm
disc

Tyres: Front is 130/60ZR16
Rear is 160/60ZR16

Dimensions:
Length: 2 030 mm
Width: 655 mm
Wheelbase: 1 450 mm
Clearance: 165 mm
Seat height: 780 mm
Dry weight: 195 kg
Fuel tank: 22 litres

Performance:
Top speed: 204 km/h
Fuel consumption: 7 l/100 km

Features: Fully enclosed
aerodynamic bodywork.

Manufacturer: Cagiva-Ducati S.p.A.

DUCATI (Italy)

Model: Indiana 350

Engine: 4-str Desmo valve 90°
vee-twin
Capacity: 349 cc
Bore × Stroke: 66 × 51 mm
Compression ratio: 10:1
Carburettor: 2 × 30 mm Dell'Orto
Maximum power: 38 bhp at
9 250 rpm
Starting: electric

Transmission: 5-speed chain

Electrics: 12 v electronic
ignition with 14 Ah battery

Frame: Duplex tubular cradle

Suspension: Telehydraulic
front fork with twin rear
adjustable dampers.

Manufacturer: Cagiva-Ducati S.p.A.

Brakes: 260 mm drilled front
disc and 280 mm rear disc

Tyres: Front is 110/90V18
Rear is 140/90V15

Dimensions:
Length: 2 024 mm
Width: 930 mm
Wheelbase: 1 530 mm
Clearance: ...
Seat height: 730 mm
Dry weight: 180 kg
Fuel tank: 13 litres

Performance:
Top speed: 165 km/h
Fuel consumption: 5 l/100 km

Features: Custom styling.
Other models are 650 and 750
versions.

ENFIELD (India)

Model: 350 Bullet

Engine: 4-str ohv single
Capacity: 346 mm
Bore × Stroke: 70 × 90 mm
Compression ratio: 7.25:1
Carburettor: 26 mm Bing
Maximum power: 18 bhp at
5 650 rpm
Starting: kick

Transmission: 4-speed chain

Electrics: 12 v coil ignition with
12 Ah battery

Frame: Tubular cradle

Suspension: Telescopic front
fork with twin rear hydraulic
dampers.

Brakes: 150 mm drums front
and rear

Tyres: 3.25–19 front and rear

Dimensions:
Length: 2 120 mm
Width: ...
Wheelbase: 1 372 mm
Clearance: 140 mm
Seat height: 875 mm
Dry weight: 163 kg
Fuel tank: 15 litres

Performance:
Top speed: 120 km/h
Fuel consumption: 4 l/100 km

Features: Old British design
exported from India to Europe.

Manufacturer: Enfield India Ltd., PO 5284, Madras 600019, India.

FANTIC (Italy)

Model: 241 seven days

Engine: 2-str single
Capacity: 212 cc
Bore × Stroke: 69 × 56.5 mm
Compression ratio: 11.7:1
Carburettor: 26 mm Dell'Orto
Maximum power: 16 bhp at
5 750 rpm
Starting: kick

Transmission: 6-speed chain

Electrics: 12 v electronic
ignition

Frame: Chrome-moly steel split
end open cradle

Suspension: Telehydraulic
front fork with rear gas/oil single
shock system.

Brakes: Front disc and rear
125 mm drum

Tyres: Front is 2.75–21
Rear is 4.00–18

Dimensions:
Length: 2 080 mm
Width: 830 mm
Wheelbase: 1 330 mm
Clearance: 330 mm
Seat height: 750 mm
Dry weight: 88 kg
Fuel tank: 5 litres

Performance:
Top speed: 110 km/h
Fuel consumption: 4 l/100 km

Features: Kick starter
functions with any gear
engaged.

Manufacturer: Fantic Motor S.p.A., via Parini, 3, 22061 Barzago (Co),
Italy

FANTIC (Italy)

Model: 125 Sports HP1

Engine: 2-str LC single
Capacity: 124.4 cc
Bore × Stroke: 55.2 × 52 mm
Compression ratio: 12:1
Carburettor: 26 mm Dell'Orto
Maximum power: 21 bhp at
8 250 rpm
Starting: kick

Transmission: 6-speed chain

Electrics: 12 v electronic
ignition with 4 Ah battery

Frame: Box section cradle

Suspension: Telescopic front
fork with anti-dive and rear
monoshock system.

Manufacturer: Fantic Motor S.p.A

Brakes: Twin 240 mm front
discs and 160 mm rear drum

Tyres: Front is 3.25–16R
Rear is 3.25S18

Dimensions:
Length: ...
Width: ...
Wheelbase: ...
Clearance: ...
Seat height: ...
Dry weight: ...
Fuel tank: 13 litres

Performance:
Top speed: 140 km/h
Fuel consumption: 4.7 l/100 km

Features:

FANTIC (Italy)

Model: Trail 50 Progress 1

Engine: 2-str reed-valve LC single
Capacity: 49.74 cc
Bore × Stroke: 41 × 37.7 mm
Compression ratio: 12:1
Carburettor: 12 mm Dell'Orto
Maximum power: 6 bhp at 8 000 rpm
Starting: kick

Transmission: 6-speed chain

Electrics: 12 v electronic ignition

Frame: Chrome-moly steel split end open cradle

Suspension: Telehydraulic front fork with adjustable *Single Shock System.*

Manufacturer: Fantic Motor S.p.A.

Brakes: 185 mm front disc and rear 118 mm drum

Tyres: Front is 2.50–21
Rear is 3.50–18

Dimensions:
Length: 1 930 mm
Width: 810 mm
Wheelbase: 1 120 mm
Clearance: 350 mm
Seat height: 755 mm
Dry weight: 65 kg
Fuel tank: 3.8 litres

Performance:
Top speed: 75 km/h
Fuel consumption: 2.5 l/100 km

Features: Trial range includes models at 80 cc, 125 cc and 250 cc.

FANTIC (Italy)

Model: Oasis 50.1

Engine: 2-str LC single
Capacity: 49.6 cc
Bore × Stroke: 38.8 × 42 mm
Compression ratio: 11:1
Carburettor: 12 mm Dell'Orto
Maximum power: 7.5 bhp at
9 000 rpm
Starting: electric/kick

Transmission: 6-speed chain

Electrics: 12 v electronic
ignition with 4 Ah battery

Frame: Duplex tubular cradle

Suspension: Telehydraulic
front fork with rear gas/oil single
shock system.

Manufacturer: Fantic Motor S.p.A.

Brakes: 230 mm drilled disc
front and rear

Tyres: Front is 2.75–21
Rear is 4.10–18

Dimensions:
Length: 2 040 mm
Width: 830 mm
Wheelbase: 1 350 mm
Clearance: 320 mm
Seat height: 830 mm
Dry weight: 87 kg
Fuel tank: 18 litres

Performance:
Top speed: 85 km/h
Fuel consumption: 2.2 l/100 km

Features: Knuckle protectors,
rear parcel grid. Brake disc
protector fitted.

FANTIC (Italy)

Model: Koala

Engine: 2-str LC single
Capacity: 49.6 cc
Bore × Stroke: 38.8 × 42 mm
Compression ratio: 11:1
Carburettor: 12 mm Dell'Orto
Maximum power: 7.5 bhp at
9 000 rpm
Starting: electric/kick

Transmission: 4-speed chain

Electrics: 12 v electronic
ignition with 4 Ah battery

Frame: Duplex tubular cradle

Suspension: Telehydraulic
front fork with gas/oil mono
shock system.

Manufacturer: Fantic Motor S.p.A.

Brakes: 240 mm front disc and
220 mm rear disc

Tyres: 21–12.00 × 8 front and
rear

Dimensions:
Length: 1 930 mm
Width: 840 mm
Wheelbase: 1 280 mm
Clearance: . . .
Seat height: 790 mm
Dry weight: 100 kg
Fuel tank: 7 litres

Performance:
Top speed: 70 km/h
Fuel consumption: 3.1 l/100 km

Features: Rear parcel carrier.
Tubeless tyres.

FANTIC (Italy)

Model: Issimo KS

Engine: 2-str reed-valve single
Capacity: 49.5 cc
Bore × Stroke: 40.3 × 38.8 mm
Compression ratio: 8.6:1
Carburettor: 12 mm Dell'Orto
Maximum power: 1.5 bhp at
5 500 rpm
Starting: kick

Transmission: Single speed

Electrics: 6 v flywheel magneto

Frame: Steel tube step-thru

Suspension: Telescopic front
fork with twin rear dampers.

Manufacturer: Fantic Motor S.p.A.

Brakes: 90 mm drums front
and rear

Tyres: 2.50–16 front and rear

Dimensions:
Length: 1 700 mm
Width: 680 mm
Wheelbase: 1 100 mm
Clearance: 160 mm
Seat height: 810 mm
Dry weight: 51 kg
Fuel tank: 3.2 litres

Performance:
Top speed: 40 km/h
Fuel consumption: 1.7 l/100 km

Features: Range includes the
Multispeed and 3V Raider
models.

GILERA (Italy)

Model: 500 Dakota

Engine: 4-str 4-valve LC single
Capacity: 491.9 cc
Bore × Stroke: 92 × 74 mm
Compression ratio: 9.5:1
Carburettor: 2 × 25 mm Dell'Orto
Maximum power: 44 bhp at
7 250 rpm
Starting: electric

Transmission: 5-speed chain

Electrics: 12 v CDI ignition
with 14 Ah battery

Frame: Duplex tubular cradle

Suspension: Air-assisted front
fork with rear adjustable *Power-Drive* system.

Brakes: 260 mm drilled disc
with dual piston caliper and rear
140 mm drum

Tyres: Front is 90/90–21
Rear is 5.10–17

Dimensions:
Length: 2 210 mm
Width: 910 mm
Wheelbase: 1 480 mm
Clearance: ...
Seat height: 860 mm
Dry weight: 148 kg
Fuel tank: 22 litres

Performance:
Top speed: 160 km/h
Fuel consumption: 5 l/100 km

Features: Kick start version,
optional tubeless tyres.

Manufacturer: Piaggio & C. S.p.A., Divisione Gilera, via C. Battisti, 68,
20043 Arcore(MI), Italy.

GILERA (Italy)

Model: ER350 Dakota

Engine: 4-str 4-valve LC single
Capacity: 348.8 cc
Bore × Stroke: 80 × 69.4 mm
Compression ratio: 9.5:1
Carburettor: 2 × 25 mm Dell'Orto
Maximum power: 33 bhp at
7 500 rpm
Starting: kick

Transmission: 5-speed chain

Electrics: 12 v CDI ignition
with 12 Ah battery

Frame: Duplex tubular cradle

Suspension: Air-assisted front
fork with rear adjustable *Power-
Drive* system.

Brakes: 260 mm drilled disc
with dual-piston caliper and 160
mm drum

Tyres: Front is 90/90–21
Rear is 4.60S17

Dimensions:
Length: 2 210 mm
Width: 910 mm
Wheelbase: 1 480 mm
Clearance: ...
Seat height: 880 mm
Dry weight: 147 kg
Fuel tank: 13.5 litres

Performance:
Top speed: 145 km/h
Fuel consumption: 5 l/100 km

Features: Electric start and
tubeless tyres optional extra.

Manufacturer: Piaggio & C. S.p.A. (Gilera).

GILERA (Italy)

Model: 125KZ

Engine: 2-str reed-valve LC single
Capacity: 124.5 cc
Bore × Stroke: 56 × 50.5 mm
Compression ratio: 13.5:1
Carburettor: 26 mm PowerJet Dell'Orto
Maximum power: 26 bhp at 9 250 rpm
Starting: kick

Transmission: 6-speed chain

Electrics: 12 v CDI ignition with 5.5 Ah battery

Frame: Box section cradle

Suspension: Air-assisted front fork with anti-dive and rear alloy swinging arm *Power-Drive.*

Brakes: Single 240 mm drilled disc with dual-piston caliper front and rear

Tyres: Front is 100/80S16 Rear is 120/80S16

Dimensions:
Length: 1 950 mm
Width: ...
Wheelbase: 1 350 mm
Clearance: 160 mm
Seat height: 760 mm
Dry weight: 113 kg
Fuel tank: 13 litres

Performance:
Top speed: 143 km/h
Fuel consumption: 3.8 l/100 km

Features: Race track styling with Advanced Power Tuning System for enhanced carburation.

Manufacturer: Piaggio & C. S.p.A. (Gilera).

GILERA (Italy)

Model: 125 FastBike

Engine: 2-str reed-valve LC single
Capacity: 124.38 cc
Bore × Stroke: 56 × 50.5 mm
Compression ratio: 13:1
Carburettor: 28 mm Dell'Orto
Maximum power: 25 bhp at 8 750 rpm
Starting: kick

Transmission: 6-speed chain

Electrics: 12 v CDI ignition with 5.5 Ah battery

Frame: Box section cradle

Suspension: Telehydraulic front fork with rear single *Monodrive* system.

Brakes: Single 240 mm disc with dual-piston caliper and rear 230 mm disc

Tyres: Front is 90/90–18
Rear is 4.70–17

Dimensions:
Length: 2 180 mm
Width: 910 mm
Wheelbase: 1 385 mm
Clearance: 320 mm
Seat height: 850 mm
Dry weight: 118 kg
Fuel tank: 15 litres

Performance:
Top speed: 134 km/h
Fuel consumption: 3.6 l/100 km

Features: Electric start optional. Also available with 183 cc engine.

Manufacturer: Piaggio & C. S.p.A. (Gilera).

HARLEY-DAVIDSON (USA)

Model: FLHTC Electra Glide Classic

Engine: 4-str ohv Evolution 45° vee-twin
Capacity: 1 340 cc
Bore × Stroke: 88.8 × 108 mm
Compression ratio: 8.5:1
Carburettor: 38 mm butterfly
Maximum power: 82.5 bhp at 4 000 rpm
Starting: electric

Transmission: 5-speed belt drive

Electrics: 12 v electronic ignition with 19 Ah battery

Frame: Steel box section backbone with twin downtubes

Suspension: Air-assisted fork with anti-dive and adjustable rear dampers.

Brakes: 292 mm triple disc system

Tyres: MT90–16T front and rear

Dimensions:
Length: 2 395 mm
Width: . . .
Wheelbase: 1 598 mm
Clearance: 130 mm
Seat height: 711 mm
Dry weight: 323 kg
Fuel tank: 18.9 litres

Performance:
Top speed: 165 km/h
Fuel consumption: 5.6 l/100 km

Features: The full dress tourer, King and Queen seats, tourpack box, frame-mounted fairing with radio and cassette, intercom and weather channel monitor.

Manufacturer: Harley-Davidson International, PO Box 1109, Ridgefield, Connecticut, 06877, USA.

HARLEY-DAVIDSON (USA)

Model: FXR Super Glide

Engine: 4-str ohv Evolution 45°
vee-twin
Capacity: 1 340 cc
Bore × Stroke: 88.8 × 108 mm
Compression ratio: 8.5:1
Carburettor: 38 mm butterfly
Maximum power: 80 bhp at
4 000 rpm
Starting: electric

Transmission: 5-speed belt
drive

Electrics: 12 v electronic
ignition with 19 Ah battery

Frame: Steel box section
backbone with twin downtubes

Suspension: Telescopic front
fork with twin rear adjustable
dampers.

Brakes: 292 mm discs front
and rear

Tyres: Front is MJ90–19
Rear is MT90–16

Dimensions:
Length: 2 327 mm
Width: . . .
Wheelbase: 1 603 mm
Clearance: 135 mm
Seat height: 660 mm
Dry weight: 261 kg
Fuel tank: 15.9 litres

Performance:
Top speed: 180 km/h
Fuel consumption: 5 l/100 km

Features: Milwaukee custom
bike that mates a Sportster front
end with an Electra Glide
chassis. Buckhorn handlebars
and Fat Bob tank. Drive belt is a
Kevlar reinforced Polychain.

Manufacturer: Harley-Davidson International.

HARLEY-DAVIDSON (USA)

Model: FXRT Sport Glide

Engine: 4-str ohv Evolution 45°
vee-twin
Capacity: 1 340 cc
Bore × Stroke: 88.8 × 108 mm
Compression ratio: 8.5:1
Carburettor: 38 mm butterfly
Maximum power: 80 bhp at
4 000 rpm
Starting: electric

Transmission: 5-speed belt
drive

Electrics: 12 v electronic
ignition with 19 Ah battery

Frame: Steel box section
backbone with twin downtubes

Suspension: Air adjustable
front fork with anti-dive and
adjustable rear dampers.

Brakes: 292 mm discs front
and rear

Tyres: Front is MM90–19
Rear is MT90–16

Dimensions:
Length: 2 393 mm
Width: ...
Wheelbase: 1 643 mm
Clearance: 152 mm
Seat height: 706 mm
Dry weight: 297 kg
Fuel tank: 15.9 litres

Performance:
Top speed: 175 km/h
Fuel consumption: 5 l/100 km

Features: Digital clock and
sound system with handlebar
controls.

Manufacturer: Harley-Davidson International.

HARLEY-DAVIDSON (USA)

Model: FXLR Low Rider Custom

Engine: 4-str ohv Evolution 45° vee-twin
Capacity: 1 340 cc
Bore × Stroke: 88.8 × 108 mm
Compression ratio: 8.5:1
Carburettor: 38 mm butterfly
Maximum power: 80 bhp at 4 000 rpm
Starting: electric

Transmission: 5-speed belt drive

Electrics: 12 v electronic ignition

Frame: Steel box section backbone with twin downtubes

Suspension: Telescopic front fork with twin rear adjustable dampers.

Brakes: 292 mm discs front and rear

Tyres: Front is MH90–21
Rear is MT90–16

Dimensions:
Length: 2 327 mm
Width: ...
Wheelbase: 1 603 mm
Clearance: 135 mm
Seat height: 673 mm
Dry weight: 261 kg
Fuel tank: 15.9 litres

Performance:
Top speed: 170 km/h
Fuel consumption: 5 l/100 km

Features: Low profile teardrop tank with hand-laced leather pinstriping, custom bars, fork-mounted chrome headlight. Solid disc rear wheel.

Manufacturer: Harley-Davidson International.

HARLEY-DAVIDSON (USA)

Model: FLSTC Heritage Softail Classic

Engine: 4-str ohv Evolution 45° vee-twin
Capacity: 1 340 cc
Bore × Stroke: 88.8 × 108 mm
Compression ratio: 8.5:1
Carburettor: 338 mm butterfly
Maximum power: 80 bhp at 4 000 rpm
Starting: electric

Transmission: 5-speed belt drive

Electrics: 12 v electronic ignition with 19 Ah battery

Frame: Duplex tubular cradle

Suspension: Air-assisted front fork and twin rear adjustable horizontally-mounted gas shock absorbers.

Brakes: 292 mm discs front and rear

Tyres: MT90–16 front and rear

Dimensions:
Length: 2 383 mm
Width: ...
Wheelbase: 1 588 mm
Clearance: 135 mm
Seat height: 673 mm
Dry weight: 322 kg
Fuel tank: 15.9 litres

Performance:
Top speed: 180 km/h
Fuel consumption: 5.5 l/100 km

Features: Fifties era styling with Fat Bob tank, twin chrome passing lights, stud-trimmed leather saddle bags.

Manufacturer: Harley-Davidson International.

HARLEY-DAVIDSON (USA)

Model: XLH 1200 Sportster

Engine: 4-str ohv Evolution 45°
vee-twin
Capacity: 1 200 cc
Bore × Stroke: 88.8 × 96.8 cc
Compression ratio: 9:1
Carburettor: 40 mm cv
Maximum power: 72 bhp at
4 000 rpm
Starting: electric

Transmission: 4-speed chain

Electrics: 12 v electronic
ignition with 19 Ah battery

Frame: Duplex tubular cradle

Suspension: Telescopic front
fork with long travel rear
dampers.

Brakes: 292 mm drilled discs
front and rear

Tyres: Front is MT90–19
Rear is MT90–16

Dimensions:
Length: 2 223 mm
Width: ...
Wheelbase: 1 524 mm
Clearance: 170 mm
Seat height: 737 mm
Dry weight: 207 kg
Fuel tank: 8.5 litres

Performance:
Top speed: 190 km/h
Fuel consumption: 5 l/100 km

Features: Buckhorn pullback
bars and stepped seat. Cast alloy
wheels. Model first appeared in
1957.

Manufacturer: Harley-Davidson International.

HARLEY-DAVIDSON (USA)

Model: XL883 Hugger

Engine: 4-str ohv Evolution 45°
vee-twin
Capacity: 883 cc
Bore × Stroke: 76.2 × 96.8 mm
Compression ratio: 9:1
Carburettor: 40 mm cv
Maximum power: 55 bhp at
4 500 rpm
Starting: electric

Transmission: 4-speed chain

Electrics: 12 v electronic
ignition with 19 Ah battery

Frame: Duplex tubular cradle

Suspension: Telescopic front
fork with twin long-travel rear
dampers.

Brakes: 292 mm drilled discs
front and rear

Tyres: Front is MJ90–19
Rear is MT90–16

Dimensions:
Length: 2 223 mm
Width: . . .
Wheelbase: 1 537 mm
Clearance: 150 mm
Seat height: 679 mm
Dry weight: 210 kg
Fuel tank: 8.5 litres

Performance:
Top speed: 180 km/h
Fuel consumption: 5 l/100 km

Features: Low ride Sportster.
Optional pillion pad available.
The Sportster 883 has wire
wheels.

Manufacturer: Harley-Davidson International.

HESKETH (England)

Model: V1000

Engine: 4-str dohc 8-valve 90°
vee-twin
Capacity: 992.3 cc
Bore × Stroke: 95 × 70 mm
Compression ratio: 10.5:1
Carburettor: 2 × 36 mm Dell'Orto
Maximum power: 86 bhp at
6 500 rpm
Starting: electric

Transmission: 5-speed chain

Electrics: 12 v electronic
ignition with 27 Ah battery

Frame: Duplex tubular cradle

Suspension: Telehydraulic
front fork with twin 3-way
adjustable rear dampers.

Brakes: 280 mm triple drilled
floating disc system

Tyres: Front is 100/90V19
Rear is 130/90V17

Dimensions:
Length: 2 235 mm
Width: 712 mm
Wheelbase: 1 510 mm
Clearance: 140 mm
Seat height: 838 mm
Dry weight: 247 kg
Fuel tank: 23 litres

Performance:
Top speed: 210 km/h
Fuel consumption: 6 l/100 km

Features: Vampire model has
full fairing.

Manufacturer: Hesleydon Ltd, Eaton Neston, Towcester, Northants
NN12 7HS, England.

HONDA (Japan)

Model: GL1200A–G Goldwing Aspencade

Engine: 4-str sohc LC opposed flat four
Capacity: 1 182 cc
Bore × Stroke: 75.5 × 66 mm
Compression ratio: 9:1
Carburettor: 4 × 32 mm cv Keihin
Maximum power: 94 bhp at 7 000 rpm
Starting: electric

Transmission: 4-speed shaft drive with an overdrive ratio

Electrics: 12 v electronic ignition with 20 Ah battery

Frame: Duplex tubular cradle

Suspension: Air-assisted front and rear with TRAC, Torque Reactive Anti-dive Control, to limit front fork dip on braking.

Brakes: Unified triple disc system with dual front and single rear d-pc discs

Tyres: Front is 130/90H16
Rear is 150/90H15

Dimensions:
Length: 2 505 mm
Width: 970 mm
Wheelbase: 1 610 mm
Clearance: 140 mm
Seat height: 780 mm
Dry weight: 329 kg
Fuel tank: 22 litres

Performance:
Top speed: 175 km/h
Fuel consumption: 7 l/100 km

Features: Instrument panel has LCD readouts. On board air compressor for suspension and tyre inflation. Stereo radio cassette with auto tuning.

Manufacturer: Honda Motor Co. Ltd, 227/28, Jingumae, Shibuyaku, Tokyo, Japan.

HONDA (Japan)

Model: CBR1000F

Engine: 4-str dohc 16-valve LC
in line four
Capacity: 998 cc
Bore × Stroke: 77 × 53.6 mm
Compression ratio: 10.5:1
Carburettor: 4 × 38 cv Keihin
Maximum power: 132 bhp at
9 500 rpm
Starting: electric

Transmission: 6-speed with
chain drive

Electrics: 12 v digital
transistorised ignition with 9 Ah
battery

Frame: Steel box section
diamond

Suspension: Air-assisted front
fork with TRAC and re-designed
adjustable *Pro-Link* at the rear
with gas-charged damper.

Manufacturer: Honda Motor Co. Ltd.

Brakes: Twin front discs and
rear single disc with d-pc

Tyres: Front is 110/80V17
Rear is 140/80V17

Dimensions:
Length: 2 245 mm
Width: 725 mm
Wheelbase: 1 505 mm
Clearance: 135 mm
Seat height: 785 mm
Dry weight: 222 kg
Fuel tank: 21 litres

Performance:
Top speed: 252 km/h
Fuel consumption: 7.6 l/100 km

Features: Fully-enclosed body
design with aluminium-cast
wheels.

HONDA (Japan)

Model: VF1000R

Engine: 4-str dohc 16-valve LC
90° vee-four
Capacity: 998 cc
Bore × Stroke: 77 × 53.6 mm
Compression ratio: 11:1
Carburettor: 4 × 36 mm cv Keihin
Maximum power: 122 bhp at
10 000 rpm
Starting: electric

Transmission: 5-speed chain

Electrics: 12 v electronic
ignition with 9 Ah battery

Frame: Box section cradle

Suspension: Air-assisted front
fork with TRAC anti-dive and rear
adjustable *Pro-Link* system.

Manufacturer: Honda Motor Co. Ltd.

Brakes: Twin floating front
discs with d-pc and rear disc

Tyres: Front is 120/80V16
Rear is 140/80V17

Dimensions:
Length: 2 187 mm
Width: 735 mm
Wheelbase: 1 505 mm
Clearance: 135 mm
Seat height: 810 mm
Dry weight: 238 kg
Fuel tank: 25.5 litres

Performance:
Top speed: over 240 km/h
Fuel consumption: 8 l/100 km

Features: Endurance style
dual headlights. Full fairing.

HONDA (Japan)

Model: VF1000F2 Bol D'or

Engine: 4-str dohc 16-valve LC
90° vee-twin
Capacity: 998 cc
Bore × Stroke: 77 × 53.6 mm
Compression ratio: 10.5:1
Carburettor: 4 × 36 mm cv Keihin
Maximum power: 116 bhp at
10 000 rpm
Starting: electric

Transmission: 5-speed chain

Electrics: 12 v electronic
ignition with 9 Ah battery

Frame: Box section cradle

Suspension: Air-assisted front
fork with TRAC anti-dive and 3-
way adjustable rear *Pro-Link*
system.

Brakes: Triple 276 mm floating
disc system with d-pc

Tyres: Front is 100/90V18
Rear is 140/80V17

Dimensions:
Length: 2 270 mm
Width: 750 mm
Wheelbase: 1 549 mm
Clearance: 140 mm
Seat height: 820 mm
Dry weight: 240 kg
Fuel tank: 23 litres

Performance:
Top speed: over 230 km/h
Fuel consumption: 8 l/100 km

Features: Dual headlamps.

Manufacturer: Honda Motor Co. Ltd.

HONDA (Japan)

Model: VFR750F–G

Engine: 4-str dohc 16-valve LC 90° vee-four
Capacity: 748 cc
Bore × Stroke: 70 × 48.6 mm
Compression ratio: 10.5:1
Carburettor: 4 × 34 mm cv Keihin
Maximum power: 105 bhp at 10 500 rpm
Starting: electric

Transmission: 6-speed with O ring chain

Electrics: 12 v electronic ignition

Frame: Aluminium box section frame

Suspension: Air-assisted front forks with *Pro-Link* rear suspension and remote hydraulic pre-load adjuster.

Brakes: Twin front discs and rear single disc with d-pc

Tyres: Front is 110/90V16
Rear is 130/80V18

Dimensions:
Length: 2 175 mm
Width: 730 mm
Wheelbase: 1 480 mm
Clearance: 135 mm
Seat height: 780 mm
Dry weight: 199 kg
Fuel tank: 20 litres

Performance:
Top speed: 236 km/h
Fuel consumption: 6.4 l/100 km

Features: Race track-bred engine. Full, sculptured fairing, cast alloy wheels, halogen headlamp.

Manufacturer: Honda Motor Co. Ltd.

HONDA (Japan)

Model: VF750C–H

Engine: 4-str dohc LC vee four
Capacity: 748 cc
Bore × Stroke: 70 × 48.6 mm
Compression ratio: 10.5:1
Carburettor: 4 × 32 mm VD type
Maximum power: 88 bhp at
9 500 rpm
Starting: electric

Transmission: 6-speed
enclosed shaft with overdrive
ratio

Electrics: 12 v electronic
ignition

Frame: Duplex tubular cradle

Suspension: Telescopic front
fork and twin rear hydraulic
dampers.

Brakes: Single drilled disc
with d-pc and rear drum

Tyres: Front is 100/90H19
Rear is 150/80H15

Dimensions:
Length: 2 386 mm
Width: 800 mm
Wheelbase: 1 660 mm
Clearance: 152 mm
Seat height: 705 mm
Dry weight: 226 kg
Fuel tank: 13 litres

Performance:
Top speed: 205 km/h
Fuel consumption: 6.4 l/100 km

Features: Low rider styling
with classic teardrop tank, fully
chromed tail pipes and alloy disc
rear wheel.

Manufacturer: Honda Motor Co. Ltd.

HONDA (Japan)

Model: CX650

Engine: 4-str ohv 8-valve LC 80° transverse vee-twin
Capacity: 674 cc
Bore × Stroke: 82.5 × 63 mm
Compression ratio: 9.8:1
Carburettor: 2 × 35 mm Keihin
Maximum power: 64 bhp at 8 000 rpm
Starting: electric

Transmission: 5-speed shaft drive

Electrics: 12 v electronic ignition

Frame: Bridge type

Suspension: Air-assisted front fork with TRAC anti-dive and rear adjustable *Pro-Link* system.

Manufacturer: Honda Motor Co. Ltd.

Brakes: Twin 276 mm discs with d-pc and rear disc

Tyres: Front is 100/90H18
Rear is 120/80H18

Dimensions:
Length: 2 250 mm
Width: 760 mm
Wheelbase: 1 500 mm
Clearance: 150 mm
Seat height: 790 mm
Dry weight: 210 kg
Fuel tank: 19 litres

Performance:
Top speed: 185 km/h
Fuel consumption: 6.4 l/100 km

Features: Handlebar-mounted fairing.

HONDA (Japan)

Model: CBR600F

Engine: 4-str dohc 16-valve LC in line four
Capacity: 598 cc
Bore × Stroke: 63 × 48 mm
Compression ratio: 11:1
Carburettor: 4 × 32 mm cv Keihin
Maximum power: 85 bhp at 11 000 rpm
Starting: electric

Transmission: 6-speed with O ring chain

Electrics: 12 v digital ignition with 8 Ah battery

Frame: Steel box-section diamond

Suspension: Air-assisted front forks with TRAC and adjustable *Pro-Link* at the rear with gas-charged damper.

Brakes: Twin front discs and rear single disc with d-pc

Tyres: Front is 110/80V17
Rear is 130/80V17

Dimensions:
Length: 2 130 mm
Width: 685 mm
Wheelbase: 1 410 mm
Clearance: 140 mm
Seat height: 785 mm
Dry weight: 182 kg
Fuel tank: 16.5 litres

Performance:
Top speed: 220 km/h
Fuel consumption: 6 l/100 km

Features: Full fairing, alloy cast wheels.

Manufacturer: Honda Motor Co. Ltd.

HONDA (Japan)

Model: Transalp 600V

Engine: 4-str sohc LC 52° vee-twin
Capacity: 583 cc
Bore × Stroke: 75 × 66 mm
Compression ratio: 9.2:1
Carburettor: 2 × 32 mm VD type
Maximum power: 54 bhp at 8 000 rpm
Starting: electric

Transmission: 5-speed with O ring chain

Electrics: 12 v CDI ignition with 12 Ah battery

Frame: Lightweight box section with double loop

Suspension: Leading axle front fork with rear adjustable *Pro-Link*.

Brakes: 276 mm d-pc disc with a 130 mm rear drum

Tyres: Front is 90/90–21
Rear is 130/80–17

Dimensions:
Length: 2 280 mm
Width: 865 mm
Wheelbase: 1 530 mm
Clearance: 214 mm
Seat height: 850 mm
Dry weight: 174 kg
Fuel tank: 18 litres

Performance:
Top speed: 170 km/h
Fuel consumption: 6.2 l/100 km

Features: Frame-mounted fairing with knuckle guards, lightweight spoked wheels. Dual purpose machine, twin aluminium radiators, one fitted with electric fan.

Manufacturer: Honda Motor Co. Ltd.

HONDA (Japan)

Model: XBR500–G

Engine: 4-str sohc 4-valve RFVC single
Capacity: 499 cc
Bore × Stroke: 92 × 75 mm
Compression ratio: 9.2:1
Carburettor: 39 mm cv Keihin
Maximum power: 44 bhp at 7 000 rpm
Starting: electric and kick

Transmission: 5-speed roller chain

Electrics: 12 v CDI ignition

Frame: Semi-double cradle

Suspension: Telescopic front forks with twin rear adjustable dampers.

Brakes: Single front disc dual-piston caliper and rear drum

Tyres: Front is 100/90–18
Rear is 110/90–18

Dimensions:
Length: 2 100 mm
Width: 695 mm
Wheelbase: 1 400 mm
Clearance: 165 mm
Seat height: 780 mm
Dry weight: 157 kg
Fuel tank: 19 litres

Performance:
Top speed: 170 km/h
Fuel consumption: 5 l/100 km

Features: Big single with Radial Four Valve Combustion system for speed, economy and flexibility. Removable rear seat hump.

Manufacturer: Honda Motor Co. Ltd.

HONDA (Japan)

Model: VF500F2

Engine: 4-str dohc 16-valve LC
90° vee-four
Capacity: 498 cc
Bore × Stroke: 60 × 44 mm
Compression ratio: 11:1
Carburettor: 4 × 32 mm cv Keihin
Maximum power: 70 bhp at
10 500 rpm
Starting: electric

Transmission: 6-speed chain

Electrics: 12 v electronic
ignition

Frame: Box section cradle

Suspension: Air-assisted front
fork with TRAC anti-dive and 4-
way adjustable *Pro-Link* system.

Manufacturer: Honda Motor Co. Ltd.

Brakes: Twin front discs with
d-pc and single rear disc

Tyres: Front is 100/90V16
Rear is 110/90V18

Dimensions:
Length: 2 070 mm
Width: 760 mm
Wheelbase: 1 420 mm
Clearance: 135 mm
Seat height: 800 mm
Dry weight: 184 kg
Fuel tank: 16.5 litres

Performance:
Top speed: 200 km/h
Fuel consumption: 8 l/100 km

Features: Middleweight
sportster.

HONDA (Japan)

Model: VT500E–F

Engine: 4-str sohc 6-valve LC vee-twin
Capacity: 490 cc
Bore × Stroke: 71 × 62 mm
Compression ratio: 10.5:1
Carburettor: 2 × 32 mm cv Keihin
Maximum power: 52 bhp at 9 000 rpm
Starting: electric

Transmission: 6-speed shaft drive

Electrics: 12 v electronic ignition

Frame: Duplex tubular cradle

Suspension: Air-assisted front forks with twin rear hydraulic dampers.

Brakes: Inboard ventilated front disc with d-pc and rear drum

Tyres: Front is 100/90S18
Rear is 120/80S18

Dimensions:
Length: 2 195 mm
Width: 760 mm
Wheelbase: 1 480 mm
Clearance: 165 mm
Seat height: 790 mm
Dry weight: 177 kg
Fuel tank: 18 litres

Performance:
Top speed: 174 km/h
Fuel consumption: 6 l/100 km

Features: Electric fan radiator, handlebar fairing and Euro-sport styling, favourite machine of dispatch riders, many low maintenance features.

Manufacturer: Honda Motor Co. Ltd.

HONDA (Japan)

Model: NS400R–F

Engine: 2-str LC vee-three with dual ATAC
Capacity: 387 cc
Bore × Stroke: 57 × 50.6 mm
Compression ratio: 6.7:1
Carburettor: 3 × 26 mm flat valve
Maximum power: 76 bhp at 9 500 rpm
Starting: kick

Transmission: 6-speed close ratio with O ring sealed chain

Electrics: 12 v CDI ignition

Frame: Aluminium box section

Suspension: Air-assisted front forks with TRAC and adjustable rear *Pro-Link* system.

Brakes: Twin front discs with d-pc and single rear disc

Tyres: Front is 110/80–18
Rear is 110/90V17

Dimensions:
Length: 2 063 mm
Width: 720 mm
Wheelbase: 1 385 mm
Clearance: 135 mm
Seat height: 790 mm
Dry weight: 163 kg
Fuel tank: 19 litres

Performance:
Top speed: 209 km/h
Fuel consumption: 9.4 l/100 km

Features: NiCaSil coated cylinder walls. Automatic Torque Amplification Chamber to give smooth pulling power at all revs, automatic oil injection system, lightweight drilled disc brakes.

Manufacturer: Honda Motor Co. Ltd.

HONDA (Japan)

Model: CB350S–G

Engine: 4-str sohc 6-valve twin
Capacity: 346.2 cc
Bore × Stroke: 66 × 50.6 mm
Compression ratio: 8.3:1
Carburettor: 2 × 32 mm cv Keihin
Maximum power: 34 bhp at
9 000 rpm
Starting: electric

Transmission: 6-speed with O
ring chain

Electrics: 12 v CDI ignition

Frame: Duplex tubular cradle in
diamond pattern

Suspension: Hydraulic front
forks with twin hydraulic rear
dampers.

Manufacturer: Honda Motor Co. Ltd.

Brakes: Twin front discs with
d-pc and a rear drum

Tyres: Front is 100/90–18
Rear is 110/90–18

Dimensions:
Length: 2 110 mm
Width: 703 mm
Wheelbase: ...
Clearance: 160 mm
Seat height: 795 mm
Dry weight: 169 kg
Fuel tank: 17 litres

Performance:
Top speed: 153 km/h
Fuel consumption: 5 l/100 km

Features: Halogen headlamp,
cast alloy wheels, economy
sports bike.

HONDA (Japan)

Model: CBX250RS

Engine: 4-str dohc RFVC single
Capacity: 249 cc
Bore × Stroke: 72 × 61.3 mm
Compression ratio: 10.5:1
Carburettor: 2 × 26 mm Keihin
Maximum power: 31 bhp at
9 500 rpm
Starting: electric

Transmission: 6-speed chain

Electrics: 12 v CDI ignition

Frame: Steel tubular cradle

Suspension: Telescopic front
fork with twin rear hydraulic
dampers.

Brakes: Front disc with d-pc
and rear drum

Tyres: Front is 90/90S18
Rear is 110/90S18

Dimensions:
Length: 2 020 mm
Width: 745 mm
Wheelbase: 1 360 mm
Clearance: 175 mm
Seat height: 770 mm
Dry weight: 129 kg
Fuel tank: 15 litres

Performance:
Top speed: 165 km/h
Fuel consumption: 5 l/100 km

Features: Radial Four Valve
Combustion system to boost
power and torque.

Manufacturer: Honda Motor Co. Ltd.

HONDA (Japan)

Model: CH250–F Spacy

Engine: 4-str sohc LC single
Capacity: 244 cc
Bore × Stroke: 72 × 60 mm
Compression ratio: 9.8:1
Carburettor: 30 mm cv Keihin
Maximum power: 21 bhp at
7 500 rpm
Starting: electric

Transmission: Honda V-Matic
variable ratio with automatic
clutch

Electrics: 12 v CDI ignition

Frame: Monocoque

Suspension: Leading link forks
with twin rear hydraulic dampers.

Manufacturer: Honda Motor Co. Ltd.

Brakes: Single front disc with
d-pc and rear drum

Tyres: 4.00–10PR tubeless
front and rear

Dimensions:
Length: 1 920 mm
Width: 710 mm
Wheelbase: 1 280 mm
Clearance: 130 mm
Seat height: 750 mm
Dry weight: 122 kg
Fuel tank: 8 litres

Performance:
Top speed: 112 km/h
Fuel consumption: 3.2 l/100 km

Features: Striking
aerodynamic design with digital
instrumentation. Also available in
125 cc version.

HONDA (Japan)

Model: NS125F–H

Engine: 2-str LC single
Capacity: 124 cc
Bore × Stroke: 56 × 50.6 mm
Compression ratio: 6.6:1
Carburettor: 24 mm Dell'Orto
Maximum power: 12 bhp at
7 000 rpm
Starting: kick

Transmission: 6-speed chain

Electrics: 12 v CDI ignition

Frame: Box section

Suspension: Marzocchi front
forks with rear *Pro-Link* system.

Brakes: Single disc with dual-
piston caliper and rear drum

Tyres: Front is 3.25–16
Rear is 3.50–18

Dimensions:
Length: 2 010 mm
Width: 720 mm
Wheelbase: 1 350 mm
Clearance: 160 mm
Seat height: 720 mm
Dry weight: 107 kg
Fuel tank: 13 litres

Performance:
Top speed: 117 km/h
Fuel consumption: 4.5 l/100 km

Features: Bikini fairing and
race-type belly pan, aluminium
bean can exhaust and cast alloy
wheels. Sports styled learner
model.

Manufacturer: Honda Motor Co. Ltd.

HONDA (Japan)

Model: CB125TD–E Super Dream

Engine: 4-str sohc twin
Capacity: 124 cc
Bore × Stroke: 44 × 41 mm
Compression ratio: 9.4:1
Carburettor: 2 × 20 mm piston valve
Maximum power: 12 bhp at 10 500 rpm
Starting: electric

Transmission: 5-speed roller chain

Electrics: 12 v CDI ignition

Frame: Tubular single cradle

Suspension: Telescopic front fork with rear *Pro-Link* system.

Brakes: Single front disc and rear drum

Tyres: Front is 3.00–18 4PR
Rear is 3.25–18 4PR

Dimensions:
Length: 2 060 mm
Width: 730 mm
Wheelbase: 1 350 mm
Clearance: 180 mm
Seat height: 775 mm
Dry weight: 124 kg
Fuel tank: 14 litres

Performance:
Top speed: 118 km/h
Fuel consumption: 3.2 l/100 km

Features: Boomerang ComStar alloy wheels, tailpiece storage and front fender with built-in air guide for engine cooling.

Manufacturer: Honda Motor Co. Ltd.

HONDA (Japan)

Model: MTX125R

Engine: 2-str piston-valve LC single
Capacity: 124 cc
Bore × Stroke: 56 × 50.6 mm
Compression ratio: 7.5:1
Carburettor: 24 mm Dell'Orto
Maximum power: 12 bhp at 7 500 rpm
Starting: kick

Transmission: 6-speed chain

Electrics: 12 v CDI ignition

Frame: Steel tubular cradle

Suspension: Air-assisted leading link fork with rear adjustable *Pro-Link* system.

Manufacturer: Honda Motor Co. Ltd.

Brakes: Single front disc with d-pc and 240 mm rear drum

Tyres: Front is 2.75–21
Rear is 4.10–18

Dimensions:
Length: 2 090 mm
Width: 830 mm
Wheelbase: 1 345 mm
Clearance: 285 mm
Seat height: 845 mm
Dry weight: 99 kg
Fuel tank: 9 litres

Performance:
Top speed: 112 km/h
Fuel consumption: 4 l/100 km

Features: Trail model with rear carrier. Unrestricted versions deliver 23 bhp.

HONDA (Japan)

Model: H100S–G II

Engine: 2-str single
Capacity: 99 cc
Bore × Stroke: 50.5 × 49.5 mm
Compression ratio: 7.2:1
Carburettor: 18 mm piston valve
Maximum power: 11.15 bhp at
6 000 rpm
Starting: kick

Transmission: 5-speed chain

Electrics: 6 v flywheel magneto

Frame: Sports style with twin
down tubes

Suspension: Telescopic front
fork with twin hydraulic rear
dampers.

Manufacturer: Honda Motor Co. Ltd.

Brakes: Drums front and rear

Tyres: Front is 2.50–18 4PR
Rear is 2.75–18 4PR

Dimensions:
Length: 1 840 mm
Width: 590 mm
Wheelbase: 1 200 mm
Clearance: 160 mm
Seat height: 770 mm
Dry weight: 86 kg
Fuel tank: 10.5 litres

Performance:
Top speed: 105 km/h
Fuel consumption: 3.3 l/100 km

Features: Lightweight sports
single.

HONDA (Japan)

Model: C90–G Cub

Engine: 4-str sohc single
Capacity: 85 cc
Bore × Stroke: 47 × 49.5 mm
Compression ratio: 8.8:1
Carburettor: 16 mm piston valve
Maximum power: 7.5 bhp at
5 500 rpm
Starting: kick

Transmission: 3-speed rotary
system with automatic clutch

Electrics: 12 v CDI ignition
with 5 Ah battery

Frame: Step-thru pressed steel

Suspension: Leading link front
fork with twin rear dampers.

Brakes: Drums front and rear

Tyres: Front is 2.50–17 4PR
Rear is 2.50–17 6PR

Dimensions:
Length: 1 835 mm
Width: 660 mm
Wheelbase: 1 175 mm
Clearance: 130 mm
Seat height: 750 mm
Dry weight: 82 kg
Fuel tank: 4 litres

Performance:
Top speed: 80 km/h
Fuel consumption: 2 l/100 km

Features: Fully enclosed chain,
leg shields. Also available with
electric start and in 50 cc
version.

Manufacturer: Honda Motor Co. Ltd.

HONDA (Japan)

Model: NH80MD–H

Engine: 2-str single
Capacity: 79 cc
Bore × Stroke: 48 × 44 mm
Compression ratio: 7:1
Carburettor: 16 mm slide
Maximum power: 6.6 bhp at
6 500 rpm
Starting: electric

Transmission: Honda V-Matic
variable ratio with automatic
clutch

Electrics: 12 v CDI ignition

Frame: Monocoque

Suspension: Leading link fork
rear single damper.

Manufacturer: Honda Motor Co. Ltd.

Brakes: Drums front and rear

Tyres: 3.50–10 front and rear

Dimensions:
Length: 1 675 mm
Width: 665 mm
Wheelbase: 1 170 mm
Clearance: 110 mm
Seat height: 710 mm
Dry weight: 74 kg
Fuel tank: 5.3 litres

Performance:
Top speed: 75 km/h
Fuel consumption: 3.5 l/100 km

Features: Aluminium cast
wheels, fitted rear carrier,
lockable luggage compartment.
The Vision is also available as a
50 cc model.

HONDA (Japan)

Model: NT50–H Mini Vision

Engine: 2-str single
Capacity: 49 cc
Bore × Stroke: 44 × 39.3 mm
Compression ratio: 7:1
Carburettor: 12 mm slide
Maximum power: 3.5 bhp at
6 000 rpm
Starting: kick

Transmission: Honda V-Matic
variable ratio with automatic
clutch

Electrics: 12 v CDI ignition

Frame: Step-thru pressed steel

Suspension: Telescopic front
fork with rear single damper.

Manufacturer: Honda Motor Co. Ltd.

Brakes: Drums front and rear

Tyres: 2.50–10 at front and rear

Dimensions:
Length: 1 495 mm
Width: 590 mm
Wheelbase: 1 065 mm
Clearance: 105 mm
Seat height: 690 mm
Dry weight: 35 kg
Fuel tank: 2.5 litres

Performance:
Top speed: 50 km/h
Fuel consumption: 1.2 l/100 km

Features: Sealed for life
battery and automatic oil
injection. Rear shopping bag
carrier.

HONDA (Japan)

Model: MT50S–G Sports

Engine: 2-str single
Capacity: 49 cc
Bore × Stroke: 39 × 41.4 mm
Compression ratio: 7.6:1
Carburettor: 12 mm slide
Maximum power: 3 bhp at
5 000 rpm
Starting: kick

Transmission: 5-speed chain

Electrics: 12 v CDI ignition

Frame: Moto cross style

Suspension: Telescopic front
fork with twin rear hydraulic
dampers.

Manufacturer: Honda Motor Co. Ltd.

Brakes: Drums front and rear

Tyres: Front is 2.50–19
Rear is 3.00–16

Dimensions:
Length: 1 905 mm
Width: 780 mm
Wheelbase: 1 240 mm
Clearance: 220 mm
Seat height: 790 mm
Dry weight: 78 kg
Fuel tank: 6.8 litres

Performance:
Top speed: 55 km/h
Fuel consumption: 2 l/100 km

Features: Automatic oil
injection system, off-road styling.

HONDA (Japan)

Model: SH50–H City Express

Engine: 2-str single
Capacity: 49.4 cc
Bore × Stroke: 44 × 39.3 mm
Compression ratio: 7:1
Carburettor: 12 mm slide
Maximum power: 3.1 bhp at
5 500 rpm
Starting: electric

Transmission: Honda V-Matic
variable ratio with automatic
clutch

Electrics: 12 v CDI ignition

Frame: Step-thru, flat floor
design

Suspension: Telescopic front
fork with twin rear hydraulic
dampers.

Manufacturer: Honda Motor Co. Ltd.

Brakes: Drums front and rear

Tyres: Front is 2.50–16
Rear is 2.75–16

Dimensions:
Length: 1 818 mm
Width: 694 mm
Wheelbase: 1 210 mm
Clearance: 140 mm
Seat height: 750 mm
Dry weight: 69.8 kg
Fuel tank: 4.5 litres

Performance:
Top speed: 50 km/h
Fuel consumption: 1.5 l/100 km

Features: Full cover leg
shields, fitted rear carrier.

HONDA (Japan)

Model: PA50–VCH Camino

Engine: 2-str single
Capacity: 49 cc
Bore × Stroke: 40 × 39.6 mm
Compression ratio: 6.7:1
Carburettor: 12 mm slide
Maximum power: 2.3 bhp at
5 500 rpm
Starting: pedal

Transmission: Honda V-Matic
variable ratio with automatic
clutch

Electrics: 6 v flywheel magneto

Frame: Pressed steel spine

Suspension: Telescopic front
fork and twin rear dampers.

Manufacturer: Honda Motor Co. Ltd.

Brakes: Drums front and rear

Tyres: 2.00–17 front and rear

Dimensions:
Length: 1 650 mm
Width: 620 mm
Wheelbase: 1 055 mm
Clearance: 120 mm
Seat height: 775 mm
Dry weight: 46.5 kg
Fuel tank: 3 litres

Performance:
Top speed: 48 km/h
Fuel consumption: 1.2 l/100 km

Features: Fully enclosed
transmission. Adjustable seat
height. Rear carrier.

HOREX (West Germany)

Model: Columbus 600

Engine: 4-str Rotax sohc
4-valve single
Capacity: 562 cc
Bore × Stroke: 94 × 81 mm
Compression ratio: 9.6:1
Carburettor: 40 mm Bing
Maximum power: 50 bhp
Starting: electric/kick

Transmission: 5-speed chain

Electrics: 12 electronic ignition

Frame: Chrome-moly tubular
space cradle

Suspension: Air-assisted front
fork with adjustable rear
monoshock system.

Brakes: Twin 280 mm floating
discs with 260 mm rear disc

Tyres: Front is 110/90V16
Rear is 130/90V16

Dimensions:
Length: ...
Width: ...
Wheelbase: 1 430 mm
Clearance: ...
Seat height: ...
Dry weight: 140 kg
Fuel tank: 17 litres

Performance:
Top speed: ...
Fuel consumption: ...

Features:

Manufacturer: ZR-bajaj Motorfahrzeuge Vertriebsges. fur Europa
mbH, D-6149 Hammelbach, Odenwald, West Germany.

HRD (Italy)

Model: WH125 Road

Engine: 2-str rotary valve LC single
Capacity: 124.6 cc
Bore × Stroke: 56 × 50.6 mm
Compression ratio: 16:1
Carburettor: 28 mm Dell'Orto
Maximum power: 24 bhp
Starting: electric

Transmission: 6-speed chain

Electrics: 12 v electronic ignition

Frame: Chrome-moly steel cradle

Suspension: Telehydraulic front fork with rear single monoshock system.

Brakes: 260 mm front disc and 160 mm rear drum

Tyres: Front is 3.00–18
Rear is 120/90–16

Dimensions:
Length: 2 000 mm
Width: 680 mm
Wheelbase: 1 360 mm
Clearance: 175 mm
Seat height: 810 mm
Dry weight: 105 kg
Fuel tank: 9.5 litres

Performance:
Top speed: 135 km/h
Fuel consumption: 4 l/100 km

Features: Silver Horse and Red Horse are fully-faired versions.

Manufacturer: HRD Motor S.p.A., via G. Puccini, 15, 20028 S. Vittore Olona (MI), Italy.

HUSQVARNA (Sweden)

Model: 510

Engine: 4-str sohc 4-valve single
Capacity: 503 cc
Bore × Stroke: 91.5 × 76.5 mm
Compression ratio: 9.5:1
Carburettor: 40 mm Dell 'Orto
Maximum power: ...
Starting: kick

Transmission: 6-speed chain

Electrics: 12 v electronic ignition

Frame: Chrome-moly steel cradle

Suspension: Leading axle air fork with rear adjustable *Öhlins* monoshock system.

Brakes: 230 mm front disc and 160 mm rear drum

Tyres: Front is 3.00–21
Rear is 4.50–18

Dimensions:
Length: 2 220 mm
Width: ...
Wheelbase: 1 480 mm
Clearance: 345 mm
Seat height: 940 mm
Dry weight: 117 kg
Fuel tank: 9 litres

Performance:
Top speed: ...
Fuel consumption: ...

Features: Enduro range includes 430 Auto, 400, 240 and 125 models.

Manufacturer: Husqvarna Motorcyklar AB, Box 103 S, 59900 Ödeshög, Sweden.

JAWA (Czechoslovakia)

Model: TS350

Engine: 2-str single with aluminium alloy cylinders
Capacity: 343.47 cc
Bore × Stroke: 58 × 65 mm
Compression ratio: 10.2:1
Carburettor: 28 mm Jikov
Maximum power: 25.8 bhp at 5 250 rpm
Starting: kick

Transmission: 4-speed chain

Electrics: 12 v coil ignition with 5 Ah battery

Frame: Tubular cradle

Suspension: Telescopic front fork with twin adjustable rear dampers.

Brakes: 160 mm drums front and rear

Tyres: Front is 3.25–18M10
Rear is 3.50–18M9

Dimensions:
Length: 2 080 mm
Width: 710 mm
Wheelbase: 1 350 mm
Clearance: 130 mm
Seat height: 810 mm
Dry weight: 166 kg
Fuel tank: 17 litres

Performance:
Top speed: 125 km/h
Fuel consumption: 4.2 l/100 km

Features: Can be fitted with Velorex sidecar.

Manufacturer: Jawa Týnec nad Sázavou, Čzechoslovakia.

KAWASAKI (Japan)

Model: VN1500 Vulcan

Engine: 4-str sohc 8-valve LC
50° vee-twin
Capacity: 1 470 cc
Bore × Stroke: 102 × 90 mm
Compression ratio: 9:1
Carburettor: 2 × 36 mm cv Keihin
Maximum power: 72 bhp at
4 000 rpm
Starting: electric

Transmission: 4-speed shaft
drive

Electrics: 12 v digital ignition
with 20 Ah battery

Frame: Steel double cradle

Suspension: Telescopic front
fork with twin rear 5-way
adjustable shocks.

Brakes: 266 mm full floater
disc front and rear

Tyres: Front is 100/90–19
Rear is 150/90–15

Dimensions:
Length: 2 390 mm
Width: 895 mm
Wheelbase: 1 630 mm
Clearance: 160 mm
Seat height: 745 mm
Dry weight: 249 kg
Fuel tank: 12 litres

Performance:
Top speed: . . .
Fuel consumption: . . .

Features: World's largest vee-
twin. Traditional custom styling
with chrome and buffed
aluminium parts. Pullback bars
and teardrop tank.

Manufacturer: Kawasaki Heavy Industries Ltd, 1-1 Kawasaki-cho,
Akashi-city 673, Hyogo, Japan.

KAWASAKI (Japan)

Model: Z1300

Engine: 4-str dohc LC in-line six
Capacity: 1 286 cc
Bore × Stroke: 62 × 71 mm
Compression ratio: 9.9:1
Carburettor: Digital fuel injection
Maximum power: 130 bhp at
8 000 rpm
Starting: electric

Transmission: 5-speed shaft
drive

Electrics: 12 v electronic
ignition with 20 Ah battery

Frame: Duplex tubular cradle

Suspension: Air-assisted front
fork with 4-way adjustable twin
rear air shocks.

Brakes: Twin 260 mm drilled
discs and a 250 mm rear disc

Tyres: Front is 110/90V18
Rear is 130/90V17

Dimensions:
Length: 2 335 mm
Width: 855 mm
Wheelbase: 1 580 mm
Clearance: 145 mm
Seat height: 835 mm
Dry weight: 294 kg
Fuel tank: 27 litres

Performance:
Top speed: 230 km/h
Fuel consumption: 8 l/100 km

Features: Cast alloy wheels
with tubeless tyres.

Manufacturer: Kawasaki Heavy Industries Ltd.

KAWASAKI (Japan)

Model: GPZ1000RX

Engine: 4-str dohc 16-valve LC in-line four
Capacity: 997 cc
Bore × Stroke: 74 × 58 mm
Compression ratio: 10.2:1
Carburettor: 4 × 36 mm Keihin
Maximum power: 125 bhp at 9 500 rpm
Starting: electric

Transmission: 6-speed chain

Electrics: 12 v electronic ignition with 14 Ah battery

Frame: Box section cradle

Suspension: Air-assisted front fork with anti-dive and 4-way adjustable *Uni-Trak* monoshock system.

Brakes: 280 mm full floating discs with a 260 mm rear disc

Tyres: Front is 120/80V16
Rear is 150/80V16

Dimensions:
Length: 2 230 mm
Width: 725 mm
Wheelbase: 1 505 mm
Clearance: 140 mm
Seat height: 805 mm
Dry weight: 238 kg
Fuel tank: 21 litres

Performance:
Top speed: over 250 km/h
Fuel consumption: 8 l/100 km

Features: Semi-flat slide carbs. Radial tyres.

Manufacturer: Kawasaki Heavy Industries Ltd.

KAWASAKI (Japan)

Model: 1000GTR

Engine: 4-str dohc 16-valve LC
in-line four
Capacity: 997 cc
Bore × Stroke: 74 × 58 mm
Compression ratio: 10.2:1
Carburettor: 4 × 32 mm Keihin
Maximum power: 110 bhp at
9 500 rpm
Starting: electric

Transmission: 6-speed shaft
drive

Electrics: 12 v electronic
ignition with 18 Ah battery

Frame: Steel diamond

Suspension: Air-assisted front
fork with *Uni-Trak* rear
monoshock system.

Brakes: 270 mm twin floating
discs and a 280 mm rear disc

Tyres: Front is 110/80V18
Rear is 150/80V16

Dimensions:
Length: 2 290 mm
Width: 760 mm
Wheelbase: 1 555 mm
Clearance: 140 mm
Seat height: 815 mm
Dry weight: 258 kg
Fuel tank: 28.5 litres

Performance:
Top speed: 210 km/h
Fuel consumption: 7 l/100 km

Features: Sports tourer with
factory-fitted panniers and tall
windscreen.

Manufacturer: Kawasaki Heavy Industries Ltd.

KAWASAKI (Japan)

Model: ZL1000 Eliminator

Engine: 4-str dohc 16-valve LC in-line four
Capacity: 997 cc
Bore × Stroke: 74 × 58 mm
Compression ratio: 10.2:1
Carburettor: 4 × 34 mm cv Keihin
Maximum power: 110 bhp at 9 000 rpm
Starting: electric

Transmission: 6-speed shaft drive

Electrics: 12 v electronic ignition with 14 Ah battery

Frame: Steel double cradle

Suspension: Telescopic front fork with twin rear adjustable dampers.

Brakes: 280 mm dual disc with single piston caliper and 270 mm rear disc

Tyres: Front is 100/90V18
Rear is 160/80V15

Dimensions:
Length: 2 330 mm
Width: 805 mm
Wheelbase: 1 615 mm
Clearance: 155 mm
Seat height: 750 mm
Dry weight: 244 kg
Fuel tank: 18.5 litres

Performance:
Top speed: 220 km/h
Fuel consumption: 6.5 l/100 km

Features: Drag racer styling with twin megaphone silencers.

Manufacturer: Kawasaki Heavy Industries Ltd.

KAWASAKI (Japan)

Model: GPZ900R

Engine: 4-str dohc 16-valve LC in-line four
Capacity: 908 cc
Bore × Stroke: 72.5 × 55 mm
Compression ratio: 11:1
Carburettor: 4 × 34 mm cv Keihin
Maximum power: 110 bhp at 9 000 rpm
Starting: electric

Transmission: 6-speed chain

Electrics: 12 v electronic ignition with 14 Ah battery

Frame: Steel tubular diamond

Suspension: Telehydraulic front fork with anti-dive and AVDS with rear adjustable *Uni-Trak* system.

Brakes: Twin 280 mm floating discs and 270 mm rear disc

Tyres: Front is 120/80V16
Rear is 130/80V18

Dimensions:
Length: 2 200 mm
Width: 750 mm
Wheelbase: 1 495 mm
Clearance: 140 mm
Seat height: 780 mm
Dry weight: 228 kg
Fuel tank: 22 litres

Performance:
Top speed: 250 km/h
Fuel consumption: 6.3 l/100 km

Features: Automatic Variable Damping System on front fork. Fitted tubeless tyres.

Manufacturer: Kawasaki Heavy Industries Ltd.

105

KAWASAKI (Japan)

Model: GPZ750R

Engine: 4-str dohc 16-valve LC in-line four
Capacity: 748 cc
Bore × Stroke: 68 × 51.5 mm
Compression ratio: 11.2:1
Carburettor: 4 × 34 mm cv Keihin
Maximum power: 106 bhp at 10 500 rpm
Starting: electric

Transmission: 6-speed chain

Electrics: 12 v electronic ignition with 14 Ah battery

Frame: Steel tubular diamond

Suspension: Telehydraulic front fork with ESCS and rear adjustable *Uni-Trak* system.

Brakes: Twin 280 mm discs and single 270 mm disc with dual-piston calipers

Tyres: Front is 110/90V16
Rear is 140/70V18

Dimensions:
Length: 2 170 mm
Width: 715 mm
Wheelbase: 1 460 mm
Clearance: 150 mm
Seat height: 775 mm
Dry weight: 195 kg
Fuel tank: 21 litres

Performance:
Top speed: 230 km/h
Fuel consumption: 6.5 l/100 km

Features: Lightweight flat carbs. Electric Suspension Control System incorporating anti-dive.

Manufacturer: Kawasaki Heavy Industries Ltd.

KAWASAKI (Japan)

Model: GPZ750

Engine: 4-str dohc in-line four
Capacity: 738 cc
Bore × Stroke: 66 × 54 mm
Compression ratio: 9.5:1
Carburettor: 4 × 34 mm Keihin
Maximum power: 86 bhp at
9 500 rpm
Starting: electric

Transmission: 5-speed chain

Electrics: 12 v electronic
ignition with 14 Ah battery

Frame: Steel double cradle

Suspension: Air-assisted front
fork with anti-dive and rear
adjustable *Uni-Trak* system.

Manufacturer: Kawasaki Heavy Industries Ltd.

Brakes: 230 mm triple drilled
disc system

Tyres: Front is 110/90V18
Rear is 130/90V17

Dimensions:
Length: 2 215 mm
Width: 770 mm
Wheelbase: 1 490 mm
Clearance: 150 mm
Seat height: 800 mm
Dry weight: 224 kg
Fuel tank: 19 litres

Performance:
Top speed: 215 km/h
Fuel consumption: 6.6 l/100 km

Features: Euro-styled, air-
cooled GPZ.

KAWASAKI (Japan)

Model: GT750

Engine: 4-str dohc in-line four
Capacity: 738 cc
Bore × Stroke: 66 × 54 mm
Compression ratio: 9.5:1
Carburettor: 4 × 34 mm Mikuni
Maximum power: 78 bhp at
9 500 rpm
Starting: electric

Transmission: 5-speed shaft
drive

Electrics: 12 v electronic
ignition with 14 Ah battery

Frame: Steel double cradle

Suspension: Air-assisted front
fork with twin 4-way air-
adjustable rear shocks.

Brakes: 260 mm triple drilled
disc system

Tyres: Front is 100/90H19
Rear is 120/90H18

Dimensions:
Length: 2 255 mm
Width: 760 mm
Wheelbase: 1 480 mm
Clearance: 150 mm
Seat height: 800 mm
Dry weight: 220 kg
Fuel tank: 24.3 litres

Performance:
Top speed: 205 km/h
Fuel consumption: 6 l/100 km

Features: Touring model with
rear carrier.

Manufacturer: Kawasaki Heavy Industries Ltd.

KAWASAKI (Japan)

Model: VN750

Engine: 4-str dohc LC 50° vee-twin
Capacity: 749 cc
Bore × Stroke: 84.9 × 66.2 mm
Compression ratio: 10.3:1
Carburettor: 2 × 34 mm Keihin
Maximum power: 66 bhp at 7 500 rpm
Starting: electric

Transmission: 5-speed shaft drive

Electrics: 12 v electronic ignition with 14 Ah battery

Frame: Steel double cradle

Suspension: Air-adjustable front fork with twin air-adjustable rear shocks.

Brakes: 220 mm twin drilled discs with 180 mm rear drum

Tyres: Front is 100/90H19
Rear is 150/90H15

Dimensions:
Length: 2 210 mm
Width: 820 mm
Wheelbase: 1 585 mm
Clearance: 140 mm
Seat height: 750 mm
Dry weight: 223 kg
Fuel tank: 13.5 litres

Performance:
Top speed: 185 km/h
Fuel consumption: 6 l/100 km

Features: Twin spark plugs to each cylinder.

Manufacturer: Kawasaki Heavy Industries Ltd.

KAWASAKI (Japan)

Model: KLR650

Engine: 4-str dohc 4-valve LC single
Capacity: 651 cc
Bore × Stroke: 100 × 83 mm
Compression ratio: 9.5:1
Carburettor: 40 mm cv Keihin
Maximum power: 48 bhp at 6 500 rpm
Starting: electric

Transmission: 5-speed chain

Electrics: 12 v electronic ignition with 14 Ah battery

Frame: Tubular double cradle

Suspension: Air-adjustable front fork with rear *Uni-Trak* system.

Brakes: 260 mm drilled front disc with 230 mm rear disc

Tyres: Front is 90/90–21
Rear is 130/80–17

Dimensions:
Length: 2 250 mm
Width: 940 mm
Wheelbase: 1 495 mm
Clearance: 240 mm
Seat height: 890 mm
Dry weight: 153 kg
Fuel tank: 23 litres

Performance:
Top speed: 160 km/h
Fuel consumption: 5.8 l/100 km

Features: Cockpit fairing with knuckle protectors and rear carrier. Paris-Dakar styling.

Manufacturer: Kawasaki Heavy Industries Ltd.

KAWASAKI (Japan)

Model: GPX600R

Engine: 4-str dohc 16-valve LC
in-line four
Capacity: 592 cc
Bore × Stroke: 60 × 52.4 mm
Compression ratio: 11.7:1
Carburettor: 4 × 34 cv Keihin
Maximum power: 85 bhp at
11 000 rpm
Starting: electric

Transmission: 6-speed chain

Electrics: 12 v electronic
ignition with 12 Ah battery

Frame: Alloy box section
diamond

Suspension: Telehydraulic
front fork with ESCS anti-dive
and rear gas shock *Uni-Trak*
system.

Brakes: 260 mm twin disc and
240 mm rear disc with BAC

Tyres: Front is 100/80V16
Rear is 130/90V16

Dimensions:
Length: 2 140 mm
Width: 670 mm
Wheelbase: 1 430 mm
Clearance: 115 mm
Seat height: 755 mm
Dry weight: 180 kg
Fuel tank: 18 litres

Performance:
Top speed: over 230 km/h
Fuel consumption: ...

Features: Balanced Actuation
Calipers and light steel and
aluminium frame part of weight
reductions. Tubeless tyres. Fully-
streamlined fairing.

Manufacturer: Kawasaki Heavy Industries Ltd.

KAWASAKI (Japan)

Model: GPZ600R

Engine: 4-str dohc 16-valve LC in-line four
Capacity: 592 cc
Bore × Stroke: 60 × 52.4 mm
Compression ratio: 11:1
Carburettor: 4 × 32 mm cv Keihin
Maximum power: 75 bhp at 10 500 rpm
Starting: electric

Transmission: 6-speed chain

Electrics: 12 v electronic ignition with 12 Ah battery

Frame: Box section cradle

Suspension: Telehydraulic front fork with AVDS anti-dive and rear *Uni-Trak* system.

Brakes: 270 mm twin disc and 250 mm rear disc with dual-piston calipers

Tyres: Front is 110/90V16
Rear is 130/90V16

Dimensions:
Length: 2 140 mm
Width: 670 mm
Wheelbase: 1 430 mm
Clearance: 140 mm
Seat height: 770 mm
Dry weight: 195 kg
Fuel tank: 18 litres

Performance:
Top speed: 215 km/h
Fuel consumption: 6 l/100 km

Features: Fitted tubeless tyres, styling features box section space frame. Ninja middleweight.

Manufacturer: Kawasaki Heavy Industries Ltd.

KAWASAKI (Japan)

Model: GT550

Engine: 4-str dohc in-line four
Capacity: 553 cc
Bore × Stroke: 58 × 52.4 mm
Compression ratio: 9.5:1
Carburettor: 4 × 26 mm Tekei
Maximum power: 56 bhp at
9 000 rpm
Starting: electric

Transmission: 5-speed shaft
drive

Electrics: 12 v electronic
ignition with 12 Ah battery

Frame: Steel double cradle

Suspension: Air adjustable
front fork with 4-way adjustable
twin rear dampers.

Brakes: 240 mm twin disc and
180 mm rear drum

Tyres: Front is 3.25H19
Rear is 4.00H18

Dimensions:
Length: 2 230 mm
Width: 755 mm
Wheelbase: 1 475 mm
Clearance: 155 mm
Seat height: 800 mm
Dry weight: 201 kg
Fuel tank: 21.5 litres

Performance:
Top speed: 180 km/h
Fuel consumption: 5 l/100 km

Features: Cast alloy wheels
and tubeless tyres.

Manufacturer: Kawasaki Heavy Industries Ltd.

KAWASAKI (Japan)

Model: GPZ500S

Engine: 4-str dohc 8-valve LC
parallel twin
Capacity: 498 cc
Bore × Stroke: 74 × 58 mm
Compression ratio: 10.8:1
Carburettor: 2 × 34 mm cv Keihin
Maximum power: 60 bhp at
9 800 rpm
Starting: electric

Transmission: 6-speed chain

Electrics: 12 v electronic
ignition with 14 Ah battery

Frame: Box section cradle

Suspension: Telehydraulic
front fork with adjustable rear
Uni-Trak system.

Brakes: 280 mm full floater
disc and 160 mm rear drum

Tyres: Front is 100/90H16
Rear is 120/90H16

Dimensions:
Length: 2 120 mm
Width: 675 mm
Wheelbase: 1 440 mm
Clearance: 120 mm
Seat height: 770 mm
Dry weight: 169 kg
Fuel tank: 18 litres

Performance:
Top speed: 205 km/h
Fuel consumption: 5.5 l/100 km

Features: Fast middleweight
model, half fairing and belly pan.

Manufacturer: Kawasaki Heavy Industries Ltd.

KAWASAKI (Japan)

Model: LTD450

Engine: 4-str dohc 8-valve LC parallel twin
Capacity: 454 cc
Bore × Stroke: 72.5 × 55 mm
Compression ratio: 10.7:1
Carburettor: 2 × 34 mm Keihin
Maximum power: 50 bhp at 9 500 rpm
Starting: electric

Transmission: 6-speed belt drive

Electrics: 12 v electronic ignition with 12 Ah battery

Frame: Steel double cradle

Suspension: Long leading axle fork with twin rear adjustable dampers.

Brakes: Twin 240 mm front discs and 160 mm rear drum

Tyres: Front is 100/90S19
Rear is 140/90S15

Dimensions:
Length: 2 210 mm
Width: 820 mm
Wheelbase: 1 485 mm
Clearance: 140 mm
Seat height: 745 mm
Dry weight: 181 kg
Fuel tank: 11 litres

Performance:
Top speed: 160 km/h
Fuel consumption: 5.5 l/100 km

Features: Custom styling.

Manufacturer: Kawasaki Heavy Industries Ltd.

KAWASAKI (Japan)

Model: GPZ305

Engine: 4-str sohc parallel twin
Capacity: 306 cc
Bore × Stroke: 61 × 52.4 mm
Compression ratio: 9.7:1
Carburettor: 2 × 32 cv Keihin
Maximum power: 36 bhp at
10 000 rpm
Starting: electric

Transmission: 6-speed belt
drive

Electrics: 12 v electronic
ignition with 9 Ah battery

Frame: Steel double cradle

Suspension: Air-assisted front
fork with adjustable rear *Uni-
Trak* system.

Brakes: Twin 210 mm front
discs and 160 mm rear drum

Tyres: Front is 90/90S18
Rear is 110/80S18

Dimensions:
Length: 2 130 mm
Width: 745 mm
Wheelbase: 1 355 mm
Clearance: 155 mm
Seat height: 770 mm
Dry weight: 147 kg
Fuel tank: 17 litres

Performance:
Top speed: 165 km/h
Fuel consumption: 4.4 l/100 km

Features: Range also includes
the 65 bhp GPZ550.

Manufacturer: Kawasaki Heavy Industries Ltd.

KAWASAKI (Japan)

Model: GPX250R

Engine: 4-str dohc LC parallel twin
Capacity: 248 cc
Bore × Stroke: 62 × 41.2 mm
Compression ratio: 12.4:1
Carburettor: 2 × 30 mm Keihin
Maximum power: 38 bhp at 11 000 rpm
Starting: electric

Transmission: 6-speed chain

Electrics: 12 v digital ignition with 9 Ah battery

Frame: Box section diamond

Suspension: Telehydraulic front fork with adjustable rear *Uni-Trak* system.

Brakes: 232 mm single floater disc and rear 207 mm disc

Tyres: Front is 100/80–16
Rear is 130/90–16

Dimensions:
Length: 2 100 mm
Width: 670 mm
Wheelbase: 1 400 mm
Clearance: 150 mm
Seat height: 745 mm
Dry weight: 138 kg
Fuel tank: 18 litres

Performance:
Top speed: ...
Fuel consumption: ...

Features: 'Hot 250' machine. Slippery aerodynamics.

Manufacturer: Kawasaki Heavy Industries Ltd.

KAWASAKI (Japan)

Model: KMX200

Engine: 2-str reed-valve LC
KIPS single
Capacity: 191 cc
Bore × Stroke: 67 × 54.4 mm
Compression ratio: 8:1
Carburettor: 26 mm Mikuni
Maximum power: 30 bhp at
8 500 rpm
Starting: kick

Transmission: 6-speed chain

Electrics: 12 v CDI ignition
with 4 Ah battery

Frame: Steel double cradle

Suspension: Leading axle fork
with rear adjustable *Uni-Trak*
system.

Brakes: 213 mm single disc
and 183 mm rear disc

Tyres: Front is 3.00–21
Rear is 4.60–17

Dimensions:
Length: 2 220 mm
Width: 855 mm
Wheelbase: 1 375 mm
Clearance: 230 mm
Seat height: 860 mm
Dry weight: 100 kg
Fuel tank: 9.3 litres

Performance:
Top speed: . . .
Fuel consumption: . . .

Features: New model –
specification provisional. Trail
range includes KLR600, KLR250
and KMX125. Kawasaki
Integrated Power-valve System.

Manufacturer: Kawasaki Heavy Industries Ltd.

KAWASAKI (Japan)

Model: AR125

Engine: 2-str reed-valve single
Capacity: 123 cc
Bore × Stroke: 55 × 51.8 mm
Compression ratio: 6.5:1
Carburettor: 24 mm Mikuni
Maximum power: 12 bhp at
8 500 rpm
Starting: kick

Transmission: 6-speed chain

Electrics: 12 v CDI ignition
with 5 Ah battery

Frame: Steel double cradle

Suspension: Telescopic front
fork with rear adjustable *Uni-Trak* system.

Brakes: Drilled front disc and
130 mm rear drum

Tyres: Front is 2.75–18
Rear is 3.00–18

Dimensions:
Length: 2 030 mm
Width: 675 mm
Wheelbase: 1 310 mm
Clearance: 170 mm
Seat height: 795 mm
Dry weight: 107 kg
Fuel tank: 11.5 litres

Performance:
Top speed: 125 km/h
Fuel consumption: 4 l/100 km

Features: Learner legal range
includes the AR80 and AR50
models.

Manufacturer: Kawasaki Heavy Industries Ltd.

KAWASAKI (Japan)

Model: KH125

Engine: 2-str disc-valve single
Capacity: 123 cc
Bore × Stroke: 55 × 51.8 mm
Compression ratio: 7.3:1
Carburettor: 22 mm Mikuni
Maximum power: 12 bhp at
8 000 rpm
Starting: kick

Transmission: 5-speed chain

Electrics: 12 v CDI ignition
with 5 Ah battery

Frame: Steel cradle

Suspension: Telescopic front
fork with 5-way adjustable rear
dampers.

Brakes: 210 mm front disc and
130 mm rear drum

Tyres: Front is 2.75–18
Rear is 3.00–18

Dimensions:
Length: 1 925 mm
Width: 745 mm
Wheelbase: 1 260 mm
Clearance: 150 mm
Seat height: 780 mm
Dry weight: 95.5 kg
Fuel tank: 13.5 litres

Performance:
Top speed: 120 km/h
Fuel consumption: 2 l/100 km

Features: Fully-enclosed
chain. Also as 100 cc version
(KH100EX) with cast alloy
wheels.

Manufacturer: Kawasaki Heavy Industries Ltd.

KAWASAKI (Japan)

Model: KE100

Engine: 2-str disc-valve single
Capacity: 99 cc
Bore × Stroke: 49 × 51.8 mm
Compression ratio: 7:1
Carburettor: 19 mm Mikuni
Maximum power: 10 bhp at
6 500 rpm
Starting: kick

Transmission: 5-speed chain

Electrics: 6v flywheel magneto
with 5 Ah battery

Frame: Steel double cradle

Suspension: Telescopic front
fork with 5-way adjustable rear
dampers.

Brakes: 110 mm drums front
and rear

Tyres: Front is 2.75–19
Rear is 3.00–17

Dimensions:
Length: 2 060 mm
Width: 850 mm
Wheelbase: 1 285 mm
Clearance: 250 mm
Seat height: 805 mm
Dry weight: 85 kg
Fuel tank: 9 litres

Performance:
Top speed: 106 km/h
Fuel consumption: 3.6 l/100 km

Features: Trail bike.

Manufacturer: Kawasaki Heavy Industries Ltd.

LAVERDA (Italy)

Model: 1000SFC

Engine: 4-str dohc 12-valve in-line triple
Capacity: 981 cc
Bore × Stroke: 75 × 74 mm
Compression ratio: 10:1
Carburettor: 3 × 32 mm Dell'Orto
Maximum power: 94 bhp at 7 900 rpm
Starting: electric

Transmission: 5-speed chain

Electrics: 12 v electronic ignition with 32 Ah battery

Frame: Duplex tubular cradle

Suspension: Telehydraulic front fork with twin rear *Marzocchi* piggyback shock absorbers.

Brakes: 300 mm drilled dual floating discs with rear 280 mm disc

Tyres: Front is 100/90V18
Rear is 120/90V18

Dimensions:
Length: 2 180 mm
Width: 650 mm
Wheelbase: 1 500 mm
Clearance: 140 mm
Seat height: 780 mm
Dry weight: 230 kg
Fuel tank: 22 litres

Performance:
Top speed: 230 km/h
Fuel consumption: 7 l/100 km

Features: Dual/single seat.

Manufacturer: Moto Laverda S.p.A., via Venezia, 30, 36042 Breganze (VI), Italy.

MALAGUTI (Italy)

Model: Strada RGT/50

Engine: 2-str disc-valve LC single
Capacity: 49.9 cc
Bore × Stroke: 38.8 × 42 mm
Compression ratio: 10:1
Carburettor: 12 mm Dell'Orto
Maximum power: 1.4 bhp at 4 300 rpm
Starting: kick

Transmission: 4-speed chain

Electrics: 12 v electronic ignition

Frame: Tubular cradle

Suspension: Telehydraulic front fork with twin rear adjustable dampers.

Brakes: Front disc and rear drum

Tyres: Front is 2.75–16
Rear is 3.00–17

Dimensions:
Length: ...
Width: ...
Wheelbase: ...
Clearance: ...
Seat height: ...
Dry weight: 75 kg
Fuel tank: 11 litres

Performance:
Top speed: 40 km/h
Fuel consumption: 2 l/100 km

Features: Malaguti range includes mopeds and enduros.

Manufacturer: Malaguti S.p.A., via Emilia Levante, 498, 40068 San Lazzaro di Savena (BO), Italy.

MALANCA (Italy)

Model: OB ONE 6M

Engine: 2-str LC single
Capacity: 124.9 cc
Bore × Stroke: 43 × 43 mm
Compression ratio: 11:1
Carburettor: 2 × 22 mm Dell'Orto
Maximum power: 25 bhp at
11 000 rpm
Starting: kick

Transmission: 6-speed chain

Electrics: 12 v electronic
ignition

Frame: Duplex tubular cradle

Suspension: Telehydraulic
front fork with anti-dive and rear
monoshock system.

Brakes: 220 mm triple drilled
disc system

Tyres: Front is 100/90–16
Rear is 100/90–18

Dimensions:
Length: 1 900 mm
Width: 600 mm
Wheelbase: 1 280 mm
Clearance: ...
Seat height: ...
Dry weight: 100 kg
Fuel tank: 13 litres

Performance:
Top speed: 150 km/h
Fuel consumption: 6 l/100 km

Features: Also available with
full GP fairing.

Manufacturer: Malanca S.p.A., via Pila, 6, 40044 Pontecchio di Sasso
Marconi (BO), Italy.

MATCHLESS (England)

Model: G80

Engine: 4-str sohc 4-valve
single
Capacity: 494 cc
Bore × Stroke: 89 × 79.4 mm
Compression ratio: 9.2:1
Carburettor: 36 mm Dell'Orto
Maximum power: 35 bhp at
7 000 rpm
Starting: kick

Transmission: 5-speed chain

Electrics: 12 v CDI ignition

Frame: Steel tubular cradle

Suspension: Telescopic front
fork with adjustable anti-dive and
twin rear hydraulic dampers.

Brakes: Single 260 mm disc
and 160 mm rear drum

Tyres: Front is 100/90H19
Rear is 110/90H18

Dimensions:
Length: 2 140 mm
Width: 680 mm
Wheelbase: 1 372 mm
Clearance: 180 mm
Seat height: 787 mm
Dry weight: 150 kg
Fuel tank: 15 litres

Performance:
Top speed: 152 km/h
Fuel consumption: 4.5 l/100 km

Features: Rotax engine.
Quickly detachable rear wheel.
Stainless steel mudguards.
Optional twin front disc brakes.
Hand-built.

Manufacturer: Matchless Motorcycles Ltd, Units 1 & 2 Silverhills
Road, Decoy Industrial Estate, Newton Abbot, Devon TQ12 5ND,
England.

MONTESA (Spain)

Model: Cota 335

Engine: 2-str single
Capacity: 327.8 cc
Bore × Stroke: 83.4 × 60 mm
Compression ratio: 9.5:1
Carburettor: 27 mm Amal
Maximum power: ...
Starting: kick

Transmission: 6-speed chain

Electrics: 6 v flywheel magneto

Frame: Duplex tubular cradle

Suspension: Telescopic front
fork with *Marzocchi* rear
monoshock.

Brakes: Drilled discs front and
rear

Tyres: Front is 2.75–21
Rear is 4.00–18

Dimensions:
Length: 2 010 mm
Width: 802 mm
Wheelbase: 1 320 mm
Clearance: 350 mm
Seat height: 805 mm
Dry weight: 86 kg
Fuel tank: 4.5 litres

Performance:
Top speed: ...
Fuel consumption: ...

Features: Most powerful of
the Montesa trial bikes.

Manufacturer: Montesa Honda, S.A., Avda. Santa Cruz de Calafell,
21–35, 08940 Cornella de Llobregat, Barcelona, Spain.

MONTESA (Spain)

Model: Impala 2

Engine: 2-str single
Capacity: 174.7 cc
Bore × Stroke: 62 × 58 mm
Compression ratio: 8.5:1
Carburettor: 22 mm Amal
Maximum power: ...
Starting: kick

Transmission: 4-speed chain

Electrics: 6 v flywheel magneto

Frame: Tubular cradle

Suspension: Telescopic front fork with twin adjustable rear dampers.

Manufacturer: Montesa Honda S.A.

Brakes: Drums front and rear

Tyres: Front is 2.75–18
Rear is 3.00–18

Dimensions:
Length: 1 940 mm
Width: 610 mm
Wheelbase: 1 240 mm
Clearance: 230 mm
Seat height: 800 mm
Dry weight: 96 kg
Fuel tank: 12 litres

Performance:
Top speed: 100 km/h
Fuel consumption: 3.3 l/100 km

Features: Also available as 125 cc model.

MOTO GUZZI (Italy)

Model: Le Mans 1000

Engine: 4-str ohv 90° vee-twin
Capacity: 948.8 cc
Bore × Stroke: 88 × 78 mm
Compression ratio: 10:1
Carburettor: 2 × 40 mm Dell'Orto
Maximum power: 82 bhp at
7 400 rpm
Starting: electric

Transmission: 5-speed shaft
drive

Electrics: 12 v coil ignition with
24 Ah battery

Frame: Duplex tubular cradle

Suspension: Telescopic air fork
with twin rear *Koni* gas shocks.

Brakes: Twin front and single
rear 270 mm floating discs

Tyres: Front is 120/80V16
Rear is 130/80V18

Dimensions:
Length: 2 160 mm
Width: 690 mm
Wheelbase: 1 514 mm
Clearance: 120 mm
Seat height: 750 mm
Dry weight: 215 kg
Fuel tank: 25 litres

Performance:
Top speed: 230 km/h
Fuel consumption: 5.4 l/100 km

Features: Integral braking
system with front and back
brake operated by the foot pedal,
Nigusil-lined aluminium engine
cylinders.

Manufacturer: Seimm Moto Guzzi S.p.A., via E.V. Parodi, 57, 22054
Mandello del Lario, Como, Italy.

MOTO GUZZI (Italy)

Model: 1000 SP II

Engine: 4-str ohv 90° vee-twin
Capacity: 948.8 cc
Bore × Stroke: 88 × 78 mm
Compression ratio: 9.2:1
Carburettor: 2 × 30 mm Dell'Orto
Maximum power: 67 bhp at
6 700 rpm
Starting: electric

Transmission: 5-speed shaft
drive

Electrics: 12 v electronic
ignition with 24 Ah battery

Frame: Duplex tubular cradle

Suspension: Telescopic air fork
with adjustable rear hydraulic
dampers.

Manufacturer: Seimm Moto Guzzi S.p.A.

Brakes: 270 mm triple floating
disc system with Integral
Braking

Tyres: Front is 110/90V16
Rear is 120/90V18

Dimensions:
Length: 2 180 mm
Width: 750 mm
Wheelbase: 1 480 mm
Clearance: 150 mm
Seat height: 750 mm
Dry weight: 220 kg
Fuel tank: 26 litres

Performance:
Top speed: 200 km/h
Fuel consumption: 5.8 l/100 km

Features: Light alloy cylinders.
Smoke-coloured screen.

MOTO GUZZI (Italy)

Model: California III

Engine: 4-str ohv 90° vee-twin
Capacity: 948.8 cc
Bore × Stroke: 88 × 78 mm
Compression ratio: 9.2:1
Carburettor: 2 × 30 mm Dell'Orto
Maximum power: 65 bhp at
6 700 rpm
Starting: electric

Transmission: 5-speed shaft
drive

Electrics: 12 v coil ignition with
24 Ah battery

Frame: Duplex tubular cradle

Suspension: Telescopic air fork
with twin rear adjustable
dampers.

Brakes: 300 mm twin front
discs and 270 mm rear disc with
Integral Braking

Tyres: Front is 110/90V18
Rear is 120/90V18

Dimensions:
Length: 2 260 mm
Width: ...
Wheelbase: 1 498 mm
Clearance: 190 mm
Seat height: 812 mm
Dry weight: 250 kg
Fuel tank: 25 litres

Performance:
Top speed: 190 km/h
Fuel consumption: 5.8 l/100 km

Features: Stateside styling
windscreen, crashbars, panniers.

Manufacturer: Seimm Moto Guzzi S.p.A.

MOTO GUZZI (Italy)

Model: 850 T5

Engine: 4-str ohv 90° vee-twin
Capacity: 844.5 cc
Bore × Stroke: 83 × 78 mm
Compression ratio: 9.5:1
Carburettor: 2 × 30 mm Dell'Orto
Maximum power: 67 bhp at
7 000 rpm
Starting: electric

Transmission: 5-speed shaft
drive

Electrics: 12 v coil ignition with
24 Ah battery

Frame: Duplex tubular cradle

Suspension: Telescopic air fork
with 4-way adjustable *Koni*
dampers.

Manufacturer: Seimm Moto Guzzi S.p.A.

Brakes: 270 mm triple floating
disc system with Integral
Braking

Tyres: Front is 110/90V16
Rear is 120/90V18

Dimensions:
Length: 2 200 mm
Width: 760 mm
Wheelbase: 1 505 mm
Clearance: 150 mm
Seat height: 807 mm
Dry weight: 220 kg
Fuel tank: 26 litres

Performance:
Top speed: 200 km/h
Fuel consumption: 5.4 l/100 km

Features: Cockpit fairing,
steering damper, alloy wheels.

MOTO GUZZI (Italy)

Model: V75

Engine: 4-str ohv 8-valve 90°
vee-twin
Capacity: 743.9 cc
Bore × Stroke: 80 × 74 mm
Compression ratio: 10:1
Carburettor: 2 × 30 mm Dell'Orto
Maximum power: 58 bhp at
7 300 rpm
Starting: electric

Transmission: 5-speed shaft
drive

Electrics: 12 v electronic
ignition with 20 Ah battery

Frame: Duplex tubular cradle

Suspension: Telescopic air fork
with twin adjustable rear
dampers.

Manufacturer: Seimm Moto Guzzi S.p.A.

Brakes: 270 mm twin floating
discs with rear 235 mm disc and
Integral Braking System

Tyres: Front is 110/90H16
Rear is 120/80H18

Dimensions:
Length: 2 180 mm
Width: 787 mm
Wheelbase: 1 500 mm
Clearance: 150 mm
Seat height: 838 mm
Dry weight: 175 kg
Fuel tank: 17 litres

Performance:
Top speed: 200 km/h
Fuel consumption: 5.6 l/100 km

Features: Cockpit fairing.

MOTO GUZZI (Italy)

Model: V65 Lario

Engine: 4-str ohv 4-valve 90°
vee-twin
Capacity: 643.5 cc
Bore × Stroke: 80 × 64 mm
Compression ratio: 10.3:1
Carburettor: 2 × 30 mm Dell'Orto
Maximum power: 60 bhp at
7 000 rpm
Starting: electric

Transmission: 5-speed shaft
drive

Electrics: 12 v electronic
ignition with 20 Ah battery

Frame: Duplex tubular cradle

Suspension: Telescopic air fork
with adjustable rear gas shocks.

Brakes: 270 mm twin floating
discs with rear 235 mm disc and
Integral Braking System

Tyres: Front is 100/90V16
Rear is 120/90V16

Dimensions:
Length: 2 100 mm
Width: 700 mm
Wheelbase: 1 480 mm
Clearance: 140 mm
Seat height: 790 mm
Dry weight: 172 kg
Fuel tank: 18 litres

Performance:
Top speed: 195 km/h
Fuel consumption: 5.6 l/100 km

Features: Cockpit fairing. The
V65 series includes the V65 SP,
the V65 Florida custom and the
NTX650 trail bike.

Manufacturer: Seimm Moto Guzzi S.p.A.

MOTO GUZZI (Italy)

Model: NTX350

Engine: 4-str ohv 90° vee-twin
Capacity: 349.22 cc
Bore × Stroke: 74 × 40.6 mm
Compression ratio: 10.3:1
Carburettor: 2 × 28 mm Dell'Orto
Maximum power: 29 bhp at
8 400 rpm
Starting: electric

Transmission: 5-speed shaft
drive

Electrics: 12 v electronic
ignition with 20 Ah battery

Frame: Duplex tubular cradle

Suspension: Telescopic front
fork with twin rear gas-oil
dampers.

Brakes: 260 mm drilled discs
front and rear

Tyres: Front is 3.00S21
Rear is 4.00S18

Dimensions:
Length: 2 250 mm
Width: 900 mm
Wheelbase: 1 480 mm
Clearance: 250 mm
Seat height: 840 mm
Dry weight: 170 kg
Fuel tank: 32 litres

Performance:
Top speed: 140 km/h
Fuel consumption: 4.6 l/100 km

Features: Full
instrumentation. Dual purpose
machine, 2-into-1 high level
exhaust. Also with 70 bhp 650 cc
engine.

Manufacturer: Seimm Moto Guzzi S.p.A.

MOTO GUZZI (Italy)

Model: V35 III

Engine: 4-str ohv 8-valve 90°
vee-twin
Capacity: 346.2 cc
Bore × Stroke: 66 × 50.6 mm
Compression ratio: 10.5:1
Carburettor: 2 × 26 mm Dell'Orto
Maximum power: 38 bhp at
8 100 rpm
Starting: electric

Transmission: 5-speed shaft
drive

Electrics: 12 v electronic
ignition with 20 Ah battery

Frame: Duplex tubular cradle

Suspension: Telescopic air fork
with adjustable rear gas shocks.

Manufacturer: Seimm Moto Guzzi S.p.A.

Brakes: 260 mm twin floating
discs with rear 235 mm disc and
Integral Braking System

Tyres: Front is 100/90H16
Rear is 110/80H16

Dimensions:
Length: 2 090 mm
Width: 700 mm
Wheelbase: 1 455 mm
Clearance: 175 mm
Seat height: 775 mm
Dry weight: 160 kg
Fuel tank: 17 litres

Performance:
Top speed: 150 km/h
Fuel consumption: 4 l/100 km

Features: Series includes the
V35 Imola II and a custom bike.

MOTO GUZZI (Italy)

Model: 125 C

Engine: 2-str reed-valve LC
single
Capacity: 123.15 cc
Bore × Stroke: 56 × 50 mm
Compression ratio: 11.5:1
Carburettor: 25 mm Dell'Orto
Maximum power: 20 bhp at
8 000 rpm
Starting: kick

Transmission: 6-speed chain

Electrics: 12 v electronic
ignition with 6 Ah battery

Frame: Duplex tubular cradle

Suspension: Telescopic air fork
with adjustable *Mono-System*.

Manufacturer: Seimm Moto Guzzi S.p.A.

Brakes: 260 mm drilled disc
with 125 mm rear drum

Tyres: Front is 80/100–16
Rear is 3.50–18

Dimensions:
Length: ...
Width: ...
Wheelbase: ...
Clearance: ...
Seat height: ...
Dry weight: 110 kg
Fuel tank: 11 litres

Performance:
Top speed: over 115 km/h
Fuel consumption: 3.5 l/100 km

Features: 'Mini California'
model. 125 range includes enduro
model.

MOTO MORINI (Italy)

Model: 350K2

Engine: 4-str ohv 72° vee-twin
Capacity: 344.16 cc
Bore × Stroke: 62 × 57 mm
Compression ratio: 11:1
Carburettor: 2 × 25 mm Dell'Orto
Maximum power: 38 bhp at
8 500 rpm
Starting: electric/kick

Transmission: 6-speed chain

Electrics: 12 v CDI ignition
with 18 Ah battery

Frame: Duplex tubular cradle

Suspension: Telehydraulic
front fork with twin rear
adjustable dampers.

Brakes: Dual drilled 280 mm
discs and 240 mm rear disc

Tyres: Front is 100/90V18
Rear is 3.50H18

Dimensions:
Length: 2 080 mm
Width: ...
Wheelbase: 1 390 mm
Clearance: 170 mm
Seat height: 800 mm
Dry weight: 160 kg
Fuel tank: 16 litres

Performance:
Top speed: 165 km/h
Fuel consumption: 3.7 l/100 km

Features: Also in custom
version.

Manufacturer: Moto Morini S.p.A., via A. Bergami, 7, 40133 Bologna,
Italy.

MOTO MORINI (Italy)

Model: 125KJ

Engine: 4-str single
Capacity: 123 cc
Bore × Stroke: 59 × 45 mm
Compression ratio: 11.7:1
Carburettor: 24 mm Dell'Orto
Maximum power: 12 bhp at
10 000 rpm
Starting: kick

Transmission: 6-speed chain

Electrics: 12 v CDI ignition
with 2 Ah battery

Frame: Steel tubular cradle

Suspension: Leading axle fork
with adjustable rear monoshock.

Manufacturer: Moto Morini S.p.A.

Brakes: 230 mm front disc and
136 mm rear disc

Tyres: Front is 3.00–21
Rear is 4.10-18

Dimensions:
Length: 2 150 mm
Width: ...
Wheelbase: 1 390 mm
Clearance: 280 mm
Seat height: 840 mm
Dry weight: 112 kg
Fuel tank: 7.5 litres

Performance:
Top speed: 110 km/h
Fuel consumption: 2.9 l/100 km

Features: Rear carrier. Other
trailsters are 350 Kangeroo and
501 Camel.

MZ (East Germany)

Model: ETZ 250 with Superelastic sidecar

Engine: 2-str single
Capacity: 243 cc
Bore × Stroke: 69 × 65 mm
Compression ratio: 10:1
Carburettor: 26 mm BVF
Maximum power: 21 bhp at 5 700 rpm
Starting: kick

Transmission: 5-speed chain

Electrics: 12 v coil ignition with 5.5 Ah(9 Ah) battery

Frame: Welded box section bridge

Suspension: Telescopic front fork with twin rear adjustable dampers.

Brakes: 280 mm front disc and 160 mm rear drum

Tyres: Front is 2.75–18
Rear is 3.50–18 (sidecar 3.50–16)

Dimensions:
Length: 2 160 mm
Width: 900 mm (with sidecar 1 500 mm)
Wheelbase: 1 346 mm
Clearance: 150 mm
Seat height: 775 mm
Dry weight: 137 kg (240 kg)
Fuel tank: 17 litres

Performance:
Top speed: 130 (100) km/h
Fuel consumption: 5.5 (6.5) l/100 km

Features: Standard and De luxe versions. Passenger or trade sidecars can be fitted.

Manufacturer: MZ Veb Motorradwerk Zschopau, PSF 72, DDR Zschopau – 9360 East Germany.

MZ (East Germany)

Model: ETZ150

Engine: 2-str single
Capacity: 143 cc
Bore × Stroke: 56 × 58 mm
Compression ratio: 10.5:1
Carburettor: 22 mm BVF
Maximum power: 12.5 bhp at
5 500 rpm
Starting: kick

Transmission: 5-speed with
fully enclosed chain

Electrics: 12 v coil ignition with
5.5 Ah battery

Frame: Welded steel bridge

Suspension: Telescopic front
fork with twin rear adjustable
dampers.

Brakes: 280 mm front disc and
150 mm rear drum

Tyres: Front is 2.75–18
Rear is 3.25–16

Dimensions:
Length: 1 970 mm
Width: 900 mm
Wheelbase: 1 175 mm
Clearance: 150 mm
Seat height: 820 mm
Dry weight: 109.5 kg
Fuel tank: 13 litres

Performance:
Top speed: 105 km/h
Fuel consumption: 3.6 l/100 km

Features: A special 150 cc
engine delivers 14.3 bhp. 125 cc
model has 10.5 bhp output.

Manufacturer: MZ Veb Motorradwerk Zschopau.

NEVAL (USSR)

Model: Ural M67

Engine: 4-str ohv flat twin
Capacity: 649 cc
Bore × Stroke: 78 × 68 mm
Compression ratio: 7.2:1
Carburettor: 2 × K301
Maximum power: 36 bhp at
5 300 rpm
Starting: side kick

Transmission: 4-speed shaft
drive.

Electrics: 12 v coil ignition with
battery and dynamo

Frame: Steel double cradle

Suspension: Telescopic front
fork with twin 2-way adjustable
rear dampers.

Brakes: Drums front and rear

Tyres: 3.50–18 front and rear

Dimensions:
Length: 2 250 mm
Width: 900 mm
Wheelbase: 1 500 mm
Clearance: 125 mm
Seat height: 825 mm
Dry weight: 215 kg
Fuel tank: 18 litres

Performance:
Top speed: 150 km/h
Fuel consumption: 6 l/100 km

Features: Neutral lever fitted.
Comes as a solo or dual saddle.

Exported by: Avtoexport, 14, Volkhonka Street, 119902, Moscow,
USSR.

NORTON (England)

Model: Classic

Engine: Twin chamber air-cooled Norton rotary
Capacity: 588 cc
Bore × Stroke: n/a
Compression ratio: 7.5:1
Carburettor: 2 × 38 mm cv SU
Maximum power: 79 bhp at 9 000 rpm
Starting: electric

Transmission: 5-speed chain

Electrics: 12 v electronic ignition with 14 Ah battery

Frame: Pressed steel monocoque

Suspension: Telehydraulic front fork with twin rear *Koni* adjustable dampers.

Brakes: 280 mm triple disc system with dual-piston calipers

Tyres: Front is 100/90V18
Rear is 120/80V18

Dimensions:
Length: 2 180 mm
Width: 730 mm
Wheelbase: 1 486 mm
Clearance: 165 mm
Seat height: 762 mm
Dry weight: 227 kg
Fuel tank: 18 litres

Performance:
Top speed: ...
Fuel consumption: ...

Features: Limited edition (100), hand-built. QD alloy wheels. Enclosed drive chain.

Manufacturer: Norton Motors Ltd, Lynn Lane, Shenstone, Lichfield, Staffs., WS14 0EA, England.

NORTON (England)

Model: Commander

Engine: Twin chamber LC
Norton rotary
Capacity: 588 cc
Bore × Stroke: n/a
Compression ratio: 8.6:1
Carburettor: 2 × 38 mm cv SU
Maximum power: 85 bhp at
9 000 rpm
Starting: electric

Transmission: 5-speed chain

Electrics: 12 v CDI ignition
with 28 Ah battery

Frame: Pressed steel
monocoque

Suspension: Braced
telehydraulic front fork with twin
adjustable gas/oil dampers.

Manufacturer: Norton Motors Ltd.

Brakes: 265 mm triple disc
system with dual-piston calipers

Tyres: Front is 100/90V18
Rear is 110/90V18

Dimensions:
Length: 2 200 mm
Width: 900 mm
Wheelbase: 1 486 mm
Clearance: 165 mm
Seat height: 762 mm
Dry weight: 260 kg
Fuel tank: 23 litres

Performance:
Top speed: …
Fuel consumption: …

Features: Full fairing integral
panniers and police patrol
equipment. QD alloy wheels.

PIAGGIO (Italy)

Model: Vespa PX 200 E

Engine: 2-str rotary disc single
Capacity: 197.97 cc
Bore × Stroke: 66.5 × 57 mm
Compression ratio: 8.8:1
Carburettor: 24 mm Dell'Orto
Maximum power: 11.6 bhp at
6 000 rpm
Starting: kick or electric

Transmission: 4-speed with
direct drive to the rear wheel

Electrics: 12 v electronic
ignition

Frame: Monocoque

Suspension: Helical front
springs and double action
hydraulic dampers.

Brakes: 150 mm drums front
and rear

Tyres: 3.50–10 front and rear

Dimensions:
Length: 1 760 mm
Width: 695 mm
Wheelbase: 1 235 mm
Clearance: 150 mm
Seat height: 790 mm
Dry weight: 108 kg
Fuel tank: 8 litres

Performance:
Top speed: 110 km/h
Fuel consumption: 2.1 l/100 km

Features: Other models in
Arcobaleno range are 125E, 150E.

Manufacturer: Piaggio & Co. S.p.A., via Antonio Cecchi, 6, 16129
Genova, Italy.

PIAGGIO (Italy)

Model: Vespa T5 Pole Position

Engine: 2-str rotary-valve single
Capacity: 123.5 cc
Bore × Stroke: 55 × 52 mm
Compression ratio: 11.8:1
Carburettor: 24 mm Dell'Orto
Maximum power: 11.5 bhp at
6 700 rpm
Starting: kick

Transmission: 4-speed with
direct drive to the rear wheel

Electrics: 12 v electronic
ignition

Frame: Monocoque

Suspension: Helical front
springs and double action
hydraulic dampers.

Manufacturer: Piaggio & Co. S.p.A.

Brakes: 150 mm drums front
and rear

Tyres: 3.00–10 front and rear

Dimensions:
Length: 1 760 mm
Width: 695 mm
Wheelbase: 1 175 mm
Clearance: 150 mm
Seat height: 790 mm
Dry weight: 92 kg
Fuel tank: 8 litres

Performance:
Top speed: 100 km/h
Fuel consumption: 3 l/100 km

Features:

PIAGGIO (Italy)

Model: Vespa PK50XL

Engine: 2-str rotary-valve single
Capacity: 49.8 cc
Bore × Stroke: 38.4 × 43 mm
Compression ratio: 9:1
Carburettor: 12 mm Dell'Orto
Maximum power: 1.5 bhp at
4 100 rpm
Starting: kick or electric

Transmission: 4-speed with
direct drive to the rear wheel

Electrics: 12 v electronic
ignition

Frame: Monocoque

Suspension: Helical front
springs and double action
hydraulic dampers.

Manufacturer: Piaggio & Co. S.p.A.

Brakes: 150 mm front drum
125 mm rear drum

Tyres: 3.00–10 front and rear

Dimensions:
Length: 1 685 mm
Width: 700 mm
Wheelbase: 1 175 mm
Clearance: 140 mm
Seat height: 790 mm
Dry weight: 82 kg
Fuel tank: 5.8 litres

Performance:
Top speed: 98 km/h
Fuel consumption: 1.4 l/100 km

Features:

PIAGGIO (Italy)

Model: Si Tuttorosso

Engine: 2-str horizontal single
Capacity: 49 cc
Bore × Stroke: 38.4 × 43 mm
Compression ratio: 9:1
Carburettor: 12 mm Dell'Orto
Maximum power: 1.5 bhp at
4 500 rpm
Starting: pedal

Transmission: Single speed
automatic

Electrics: 6 v flywheel magneto

Frame: Tubular cradle

Suspension: Telescopic front
fork and twin rear adjustable
dampers.

Manufacturer: Piaggio & Co. Ltd.

Brakes: 90 mm front drum and
136 mm rear drum

Tyres: 2.50–16 front and rear

Dimensions:
Length: 1 595 mm
Width: 675 mm
Wheelbase: 1 050 mm
Clearance: 175 mm
Seat height: 750 mm
Dry weight: 53 kg
Fuel tank: 3 litres

Performance:
Top speed: 40 km/h
Fuel consumption: 1.8 l/100 km

Features: Headlamp cowl and
rear carrier. Other moped models
include Ciao Teen and
Superbravo.

SIMSON (East Germany)

Model: S70E

Engine: 2-str piston port single
Capacity: 70 cc
Bore × Stroke: 44 × 45 mm
Compression ratio: 10.5:1
Carburettor: 16 mm BVF
Maximum power: 5.6 bhp at
6 000 rpm
Starting: kick

Transmission: 4-speed chain

Electrics: 12 v electronic
ignition with 12 Ah battery

Frame: Steel single spine

Suspension: Telescopic front
fork with twin rear hydraulic
dampers.

Brakes: 125 mm drums front
and rear

Tyres: 2.75–16 front and rear

Dimensions:
Length: 1 890 mm
Width: 635 mm
Wheelbase: 1 210 mm
Clearance: 130 mm
Seat height: 760 mm
Dry weight: 84 kg
Fuel tank: 8.7 litres

Performance:
Top speed: 75 km/h
Fuel consumption: 2.6 l/100 km

Features: S51 is a 50 cc model.
S70 is a road-going version.

Manufacturer: Simson (IFA Kombinat), PSF 209, DDR- 6000 Suhl,
(East Germany).

SUZUKI (Japan)

Model: VS1400 Intruder

Engine: 4-str sohc 3-valve 45°
vee-twin
Capacity: 1 360 cc
Bore × Stroke: 94 × 98 mm
Compression ratio: 9.3:1
Carburettor: 2 × 36 mm Mikuni
Maximum power: 73 bhp
Starting: electric

Transmission: 4-speed shaft
drive

Electrics: 12 v electronic
ignition with 14 Ah battery

Frame: Duplex tubular cradle

Suspension: Telescopic front
fork with twin rear 5-way
adjustable dampers.

Brakes: 290 mm front disc and
275 mm rear disc

Tyres: Front is 110/90H19
Rear is 170/80H19

Dimensions:
Length: 2 230 mm
Width: 770 mm
Wheelbase: 1 620 mm
Clearance: 145 mm
Seat height: 760 mm
Dry weight: 244 kg
Fuel tank: 13 litres

Performance:
Top speed: 180 km/h
Fuel consumption: 6.4 l/100 km

Features: Harley-Davidson
look-alike. Electronic
decompressor assists starting.

Manufacturer: Suzuki Motor Co. Ltd., Hamamatsu-Nishi PO Box 1,
432–91, Hamamatsu, Japan.

SUZUKI (Japan)

Model: GSX1100EF

Engine: 4-str dohc 16-valve
TSCC in-line four
Capacity: 1 135 cc
Bore × Stroke: 74 × 66 mm
Compression ratio: 9.7:1
Carburettor: 4 × 36 mm Mikuni
Maximum power: 124 bhp at
8 500 rpm
Starting: electric

Transmission: 5-speed chain

Electrics: 12 v electronic
ignition with 14 Ah battery

Frame: Box section cradle

Suspension: Posi-damp front
fork with adjustable pre-load,
remotely adjustable *Full-Floater*
system at the rear.

Brakes: Triple disc system
with dual-piston calipers

Tyres: Front is 110/90V16
Rear is 130/90V17

Dimensions:
Length: 2 240 mm
Width: 815 mm
Wheelbase: 1 550 mm
Clearance: 155 mm
Seat height: 785 mm
Dry weight: 238 kg
Fuel tank: 20 litres

Performance:
Top speed: 230 km/h
Fuel consumption: 7 l/100 km

Features: Sports tourer fitted
with full fairing. Also in bare
form as GSX1100E.

Manufacturer: Suzuki Motor Co. Ltd.

SUZUKI (Japan)

Model: GSX1100FJ

Engine: 4-str dohc TSCC 16-valve SACS oil-cooled in-line four
Capacity: 1 127 cc
Bore × Stroke: 78 × 59 mm
Compression ratio: 10:1
Carburettor: 4 × 34 mm Mikuni
Maximum power: 136 bhp at 11 500 rpm
Starting: electric

Transmission: 5-speed chain

Electrics: 12 v digital ignition with 14 Ah battery

Frame: Steel double cradle

Suspension: Telescopic front fork with 4-way adjustable damping from a *Full-Floater* system.

Brakes: Triple 275 mm floating disc system with dual-piston caliper

Tyres: Front is 120/80V16
Rear is 150/80V16

Dimensions:
Length: 2 185 mm
Width: 765 mm
Wheelbase: 1 490 mm
Clearance: 130 mm
Seat height: 795 mm
Dry weight: 244 kg
Fuel tank: 21 litres

Performance:
Top speed: 250 km/h
Fuel consumption: 6 l/100 km

Features: Sports tourer with full fairing and Power Shield, an electrically operated front screen. Suzuki Advanced Cooling System.

Manufacturer: Suzuki Motor Co. Ltd.

SUZUKI (Japan)

Model: GSXR1100H

Engine: 4-str dohc 16-valve oil-cooled in-line four
Capacity: 1 052 cc
Bore × Stroke: 76 × 58 mm
Compression ratio: 9.7:1
Carburettor: 4 × 34 mm cv Mikuni
Maximum power: 125 bhp at 9 500 rpm
Starting: electric

Transmission: 5-speed sealed chain

Electrics: 12 v electronic ignition

Frame: Multi-rib aluminium box

Suspension: New Electrically Activated Suspension with adjustable pre-load and damping with rear *Full-Floater* system.

Brakes: Triple drilled disc system

Tyres: Front is 2.75V18
Rear is 4.00V18

Dimensions:
Length: 2 185 mm
Width: 765 mm
Wheelbase: 1 460 mm
Clearance: 130 mm
Seat height: 810 mm
Dry weight: 197 kg
Fuel tank: 19 litres

Performance:
Top speed: 250 km/h
Fuel consumption: 6 l/100 km

Features: Twin Swirl Combustion Chambers for improved combustion, Deca Piston Brake System (8 front: 2 rear), Suzuki Advanced Cooling System.

Manufacturer: Suzuki Motor Co. Ltd.

SUZUKI (Japan)

Model: GS850G

Engine: 4-str dohc in-line four
Capacity: 843 cc
Bore × Stroke: 69 × 56.4 mm
Compression ratio: 8.8:1
Carburettor: 4 × 32 mm Mikuni
Maximum power: 81 bhp at
8 500 rpm
Starting: electric

Transmission: 5-speed shaft
drive

Electrics: 12 v electronic
ignition with 14 Ah battery

Frame: Duplex tubular cradle

Suspension: Telescopic front
fork with twin rear adjustable
dampers.

Manufacturer: Suzuki Motor Co. Ltd.

Brakes: 280 mm triple disc
system

Tyres: Front is 3.50H19
Rear is 4.50H17

Dimensions:
Length: 2 195 mm
Width: 865 mm
Wheelbase: 1 500 mm
Clearance: 170 mm
Seat height: 810 mm
Dry weight: 243 kg
Fuel tank: 22 litres

Performance:
Top speed: 205 km/h
Fuel consumption: 6.8 l/100 km

Features: Gear shock damper
to overcome the torque reaction
of the shaft drive.

SUZUKI (Japan)

Model: GSXR750

Engine: 4-str dohc 16-valve
SACS oil-cooled in-line four
Capacity: 749 cc
Bore × Stroke: 70 × 48.7 mm
Compression ratio: 10.6:1
Carburettor: 4 × 29 mm slide
Mikuni
Maximum power: 100 bhp at
10 500 rpm
Starting: electric

Transmission: 6-speed sealed
chain

Electrics: 12 v electronic
ignition with 14 Ah battery

Frame: MR-ALBOX aluminium
box section

Suspension: Posi-damp
adjustable fork with *Full-Floater*
adjustable system at the rear.

Manufacturer: Suzuki Motor Co. Ltd.

Brakes: Deca piston braking –
300 mm twin front discs and rear
single disc

Tyres: Front is 110/80V18
Rear is 140/70V18

Dimensions:
Length: 2 105 mm
Width: 745 mm
Wheelbase: 1 455 mm
Clearance: 120 mm
Seat height: 795 mm
Dry weight: 176 kg
Fuel tank: 19 litres

Performance:
Top speed: 240 km/h
Fuel consumption: 7 l/100 km

Features: Startling
performance bike developed
from the GS 1000R endurance
racer, lightweight frame, seat
hump as optional extra.

SUZUKI (Japan)

Model: GSX750ES

Engine: 4-str dohc 16-valve
TSCC in-line four
Capacity: 747 cc
Bore × Stroke: 67 × 53 mm
Compression ratio: 9.6:1
Carburettor: 4 × 32 mm Mikuni
Maximum power: 83 bhp at
9 500 rpm
Starting: electric

Transmission: 5-speed chain

Electrics: 12 v electronic
ignition with 14 Ah battery

Frame: Box section cradle

Suspension: Telescopic front
fork with anti-dive and rear
remotely adjustable *Full-Floater*
system.

Brakes: Triple 270 mm disc
system with dual-piston calipers

Tyres: Front is 120/80V16
Rear is 130/80V17

Dimensions:
Length: 2 200 mm
Width: 735 mm
Wheelbase: 1 510 mm
Clearance: 140 mm
Seat height: 780 mm
Dry weight: 217 kg
Fuel tank: 19.5 litres

Performance:
Top speed: 200 km/h
Fuel consumption: 7.5 l/100 km

Features: Available in two
versions, the GSX750EF has a full
fairing.

Manufacturer: Suzuki Motor Co. Ltd.

155

SUZUKI (Japan)

Model: VS750GL

Engine: 4-str sohc TSCC 4-valve LC 45° vee-twin
Capacity: 747 cc
Bore × Stroke: 80 × 74.4 mm
Compression ratio: 10:1
Carburettor: 2 × 34 mm Mikuni
Maximum power: 55 bhp at 7 500 rpm
Starting: electric

Transmission: 5-speed shaft drive

Electrics: 12 v electronic ignition with 14 Ah battery

Frame: Duplex tubular cradle

Suspension: Telescopic front fork and rear adjustable twin dampers.

Manufacturer: Suzuki Motor Co. Ltd.

Brakes: Front disc and rear drum

Tyres: Front is 100/90–19
Rear is 140/90–15

Dimensions:
Length: 2 235 mm
Width: 750 mm
Wheelbase: 1 545 mm
Clearance: 130 mm
Seat height: 685 mm
Dry weight: 198 kg
Fuel tank: 12 litres

Performance:
Top speed: 170 km/h
Fuel consumption: 5.5 l/100 km

Features: Electric fan, typical Stateside styling with buffed aluminium wheelrims and many chrome components, teardrop tank.

SUZUKI (Japan)

Model: LS650FG Savage

Engine: 4-str sohc 4-valve single
Capacity: 652 cc
Bore × Stroke: 94 × 94 mm
Compression ratio: 8.5:1
Carburettor: 40 mm Mikuni
Maximum power: 30 bhp at 5 400 rpm
Starting: electric

Transmission: 4-speed belt drive

Electrics: 12 v electronic ignition with 14 Ah battery

Frame: Duplex tubular cradle, lowrider styling

Suspension: Telescopic front fork with twin adjustable rear dampers.

Brakes: 240 mm front disc with d-pc and rear drum

Tyres: Front is 100/90–19
Rear is 140/80–15

Dimensions:
Length: 2 180 mm
Width: 685 mm
Wheelbase: 1 485 mm
Clearance: 130 mm
Seat height: 660 mm
Dry weight: 159 kg
Fuel tank: 11 litres

Performance:
Top speed: 140 km/h
Fuel consumption: 6 l/100 km

Features: Side stand and grab rail. Engine derived from the 1400 Intruder. Fitted wire wheels.

Manufacturer: Suzuki Motor Co. Ltd.

SUZUKI (Japan)

Model: DR600R

Engine: 4-str sohc 4-valve
TSCC single
Capacity: 589 cc
Bore × Stroke: 94 × 85 mm
Compression ratio: 8.5:1
Carburettor: 38 mm slide Mikuni
Maximum power: 44 bhp at
6 500 rpm
Starting: kick

Transmission: 5-speed chain

Electrics: 12 v electronic
ignition

Frame: Tubular cradle

Suspension: Air-assisted front
fork with rear adjustable *Full-
Floater*.

Brakes: Front ventilated disc
and rear 280 mm drum

Tyres: Front is 100/80–21
Rear is 130/80–17

Dimensions:
Length: 2 215 mm
Width: 875 mm
Wheelbase: 1 465 mm
Clearance: 275 mm
Seat height: 890 mm
Dry weight: 136 kg
Fuel tank: 21 litres

Performance:
Top speed: 165 km/h
Fuel consumption: 6 l/100 km

Features: Enduro machine
with Paris-Dakar Rally styling.
Dual exhaust system and oil
cooler. Hand and headlamp
protectors fitted.

Manufacturer: Suzuki Motor Co. Ltd.

SUZUKI (Japan)

Model: GSX550ES

Engine: 4-str dohc 16-valve
TSCC in-line four
Capacity: 572 cc
Bore × Stroke: 60 × 50.6 mm
Compression ratio: 9.8:1
Carburettor: 2 × 30 mm Mikuni
Maximum power: 68 bhp at
10 000 rpm
Starting: electric

Transmission: 6-speed chain

Electrics: 12 v electronic
ignition with 12 Ah battery

Frame: Box section cradle

Suspension: Telescopic front
fork with anti-dive and rear *Full-
Floater* with adjustable pre-load.

Brakes: Twin 300 mm discs
with rear 220 mm disc

Tyres: Front is 100/90H16
Rear is 110/90H18

Dimensions:
Length: 2 120 mm
Width: 770 mm
Wheelbase: 1 420 mm
Clearance: 155 mm
Seat height: 785 mm
Dry weight: 194 kg
Fuel tank: 18 litres

Performance:
Top speed: 200 km/h
Fuel consumption: 5.6 l/100 km

Features: GP developed frame,
TSCC is designed to increase
power with lower fuel
consumption. E model in
standard trim and EF has full
fairing.

Manufacturer: Suzuki Motor Co. Ltd.

SUZUKI (Japan)

Model: RG500 Gamma

Engine: 2-str disc-valve LC
single
Capacity: 498 cc
Bore × Stroke: 56 × 50.6 mm
Compression ratio: 7:1
Carburettor: 4 × 28 mm Mikuni
Maximum power: 95 bhp at
9 500 rpm
Starting: kick

Transmission: 6-speed chain

Electrics: 12 v electronic
ignition with 4 Ah battery

Frame: Box section alloy cradle

Suspension: Posi-damp forks
with adjustable pre-load and
damping with adjustable *Full-
Floater* at rear.

Brakes: Deca Piston Braking –
twin disc at the front and single
rear disc

Tyres: Front is 110/90V16
Rear is 120/90V18

Dimensions:
Length: 2 100 mm
Width: 695 mm
Wheelbase: 1 425 mm
Clearance: 110 mm
Seat height: 770 mm
Dry weight: 154 kg
Fuel tank: 22 litres

Performance:
Top speed: 230 km/h
Fuel consumption: 7.3 l/100 km

Features: Road-going version
of RG500 race machine,
Automatic Exhaust Control
system, power valve and race-
type instrumentation.

Manufacturer: Suzuki Motor Co. Ltd.

SUZUKI (Japan)

Model: GS450EG

Engine: 4-str dohc 4-valve
TSCC twin
Capacity: 448 cc
Bore × Stroke: 71 × 56.6 mm
Compression ratio: 10:1
Carburettor: 2 × Mikuni
Maximum power: 42 bhp at
9 000 rpm
Starting: electric

Transmission: 6-speed chain

Electrics: 12 v electronic
ignition

Frame: Tubular cradle

Suspension: Telescopic front
fork with twin adjustable rear
dampers.

Manufacturer: Suzuki Motor Co. Ltd.

Brakes: Single 275 mm disc
and 160 mm drum at the rear

Tyres: Front is 3.00S18
Rear is 3.50S18

Dimensions:
Length: 2 085 mm
Width: 750 mm
Wheelbase: 1 380 mm
Clearance: 160 mm
Seat height: 820 mm
Dry weight: 175 kg
Fuel tank: 15 litres

Performance:
Top speed: 170 km/h
Fuel consumption: 5.4 l/100 km

Features: Re-launched
middleweight aimed at the
courier market.

SUZUKI (Japan)

Model: TS250X

Engine: 2-str piston and reed-valve with AEC LC single
Capacity: 249 cc
Bore × Stroke: 70 × 64.8 mm
Compression ratio: 7:1
Carburettor: 26 mm Mikuni
Maximum power: 31 bhp at 7 500 rpm
Starting: kick

Transmission: 5-speed sealed chain

Electrics: 12 v electronic ignition with 4 Ah battery

Frame: Duplex tubular cradle

Suspension: Air-assisted front fork with rear adjustable *Full-Floater* system.

Brakes: Ventilated hydraulic disc with rear 120 mm drum

Tyres: Front is 80/80–21
Rear is 110/80–17

Dimensions:
Length: 2 085 mm
Width: 830 mm
Wheelbase: 1 430 mm
Clearance: 290 mm
Seat height: 850 mm
Dry weight: 111 kg
Fuel tank: 12 litres

Performance:
Top speed: 125 km/h
Fuel consumption: 4.4 l/100 km

Features: Suzuki Automatic Exhaust Control valve is designed to smooth power output across the rev range. Trail bike range includes TS50 and a 125 cc model.

Manufacturer: Suzuki Motor Co. Ltd.

SUZUKI (Japan)

Model: RG250FCH

Engine: 2-str power reed LC twin
Capacity: 247 cc
Bore × Stroke: 54 × 54 mm
Compression ratio: 7:1
Carburettor: 2 × 28 mm Mikuni
Maximum power: 49 bhp at 9 500 rpm
Starting: kick

Transmission: 6-speed chain

Electrics: 12 v electronic ignition with 5 Ah battery

Frame: Aluminium box section

Suspension: Adjustable Posi-damp front fork with adjustable *Full-Floater* system at the rear.

Manufacturer: Suzuki Motor Co. Ltd.

Brakes: Deca piston system – twin drilled discs at front and single rear disc

Tyres: Front is 100/90–16
Rear is 110/80–18

Dimensions:
Length: 2 050 mm
Width: 685 mm
Wheelbase: 1 350 mm
Clearance: 155 mm
Seat height: 735 mm
Dry weight: 130 kg
Fuel tank: 17 litres

Performance:
Top speed: 186 km/h
Fuel consumption: 7 l/100 km

Features: Automatic Exhaust Control, bean can exhaust and racing fairing.

SUZUKI (Japan)

Model: GN250ER

Engine: 4-str sohc TSCC single
Capacity: 249 cc
Bore × Stroke: 72 × 61.2 mm
Compression ratio: 8.9:1
Carburettor: 34 mm Mikuni
Maximum power: 22 bhp at
8 500 rpm
Starting: electric

Transmission: 5-speed chain

Electrics: 12 v electronic
ignition with 12 Ah battery

Frame: Tubular steel cradle

Suspension: Telescopic front
fork with rear 5-way adjustable
dampers.

Manufacturer: Suzuki Motor Co. Ltd.

Brakes: Front disc and rear
drum

Tyres: Front is 3.00S18
Rear is 4.60S16

Dimensions:
Length: 2 035 mm
Width: 835 mm
Wheelbase: 1 350 mm
Clearance: 150 mm
Seat height: 740 mm
Dry weight: 129 kg
Fuel tank: 10.3 litres

Performance:
Top speed: 125 km/h
Fuel consumption: 4 l/100 km

Features: Re-launched custom
bike.

SUZUKI (Japan)

Model: GS125ESF

Engine: 4-str sohc single
Capacity: 124 cc
Bore × Stroke: 57 × 48.8 mm
Compression ratio: 9.5:1
Carburettor: 24 mm Mikuni
Maximum power: 12 bhp at
9 500 rpm
Starting: electric

Transmission: 5-speed chain

Electrics: 12 v electronic
ignition

Frame: Tubular single cradle

Suspension: Telescopic front
fork and twin rear adjustable
dampers.

Brakes: Front disc and rear
drum

Tyres: Front is 2.75–18
Rear is 3.00–18

Dimensions:
Length: 1 945 mm
Width: 710 mm
Wheelbase: 1 270 mm
Clearance: 170 mm
Seat height: 745 mm
Dry weight: 103 kg
Fuel tank: 11 litres

Performance:
Top speed: 115 km/h
Fuel consumption: 3 l/100 km

Features: Sporty lightweight.
Cockpit fairing, Twin Dome
Combustion Chamber to
increase output. Cast alloy
wheels.

Manufacturer: Suzuki Motor Co. Ltd.

SUZUKI (Japan)

Model: RG125UH

Engine: 2-str power reed LC single
Capacity: 123 cc
Bore × Stroke: 54 × 54 mm
Compression ratio: 7.4:1
Carburettor: 28 mm Mikuni
Maximum power: 12 bhp at 8 500 rpm
Starting: kick

Transmission: 6-speed chain

Electrics: 12 v electronic ignition with 4 Ah battery

Frame: Steel box section

Suspension: Telescopic front fork with rear *Full-Floater* system.

Manufacturer: Suzuki Motor Co. Ltd.

Brakes: Front disc and rear drum

Tyres: Front is 80/100–16
Rear is 90/90–18

Dimensions:
Length: 1 960 mm
Width: 650 mm
Wheelbase: 1 310 mm
Clearance: 145 mm
Seat height: 730 mm
Dry weight: 96 kg
Fuel tank: 13 litres

Performance:
Top speed: 128 km/h
Fuel consumption: 5 l/100 km

Features: Sports learner styled on the famous RG Gamma racers. Exhaust power chamber.

SUZUKI (Japan)

Model: GP100E

Engine: 2-str disc valve single
Capacity: 98 cc
Bore × Stroke: 50 × 50 mm
Compression ratio: 6.8:1
Carburettor: 22 mm Mikuni
Maximum power: 12 bhp at
8 500 rpm
Starting: kick

Transmission: 5-speed chain

Electrics: 6 v flywheel magneto
ignition with 4 Ah battery

Frame: Tubular cradle

Suspension: Telescopic front
fork with twin adjustable rear
dampers.

Manufacturer: Suzuki Motor Co. Ltd.

Brakes: Single discs front and
rear

Tyres: Front is 2.50–18
Rear is 2.75–18

Dimensions:
Length: 1 900 mm
Width: 750 mm
Wheelbase: 1 225 mm
Clearance: 145 mm
Seat height: 750 mm
Dry weight: 89 kg
Fuel tank: 9.8 litres

Performance:
Top speed: 105 km/h
Fuel consumption: 4 l/100 km

Features: Standard version
has wire wheels and drum
brakes.

SUZUKI (Japan)

Model: FR80

Engine: 2-str reed valve single
Capacity: 79 cc
Bore × Stroke: 49 × 42 mm
Compression ratio: 6.7:1
Carburettor: 16 mm Mikuni
Maximum power: 6.8 bhp at
6 000 rpm
Starting: kick

Transmission: 3-speed with
automatic clutch

Electrics: 6 v flywheel magneto
ignition with 4 Ah battery

Frame: Step-thru pressed steel

Suspension: Leading link front
fork with twin rear dampers.

Manufacturer: Suzuki Motor Co. Ltd.

Brakes: Drums front and rear

Tyres: 2.25–17 front and rear

Dimensions:
Length: 1 805 mm
Width: 665 mm
Wheelbase: 1 185 mm
Clearance: 130 mm
Seat height: 750 mm
Dry weight: 73 kg
Fuel tank: 4 litres

Performance:
Top speed: 65 km/h
Fuel consumption: 2.4 l/100 km

Features: Leg shields.

SUZUKI (Japan)

Model: ZR50SKF

Engine: 2-str piston-port single
Capacity: 49 cc
Bore × Stroke: 41 × 37.8 mm
Compression ratio: 6.8:1
Carburettor: 16 mm Mikuni
Maximum power: 2.9 bhp at
8 000 rpm
Starting: kick

Transmission: 5-speed chain

Electrics: 6 v flywheel magneto
with 4 Ah battery

Frame: Tubular cradle

Suspension: Telescopic front
fork with twin rear dampers.

Brakes: Front disc and rear
drum

Tyres: Front is 2.50–18
Rear is 2.75–18

Dimensions:
Length: 2 000 mm
Width: 745 mm
Wheelbase: 1 240 mm
Clearance: 170 mm
Seat height: 750 mm
Dry weight: 89 kg
Fuel tank: 5 litres

Performance:
Top speed: 50 km/h
Fuel consumption: 2.4 l/100 km

Features: Sports roadster
with cockpit fairing and cast
wheels.

Manufacturer: Suzuki Motor Co. Ltd.

TOMOS (Yugoslavia)

Model: BT50

Engine: 2-str single
Capacity: 49 cc
Bore × Stroke: 38 × 43 mm
Compression ratio: 7:1
Carburettor: ...
Maximum power: 4 bhp at
8 000 rpm
Starting: kick

Transmission: 5-speed chain

Electrics: 12 v electronic
ignition

Frame: Tubular spine

Suspension: Telescopic front
fork with twin oil/spring rear
dampers.

Brakes: 220 mm drilled disc
with 125 mm rear drum

Tyres: Front is 2.50–17
Rear is 2.75–17

Dimensions:
Length: 1 815 mm
Width: 695 mm
Wheelbase: ...
Clearance: ...
Seat height: ...
Dry weight: 70 kg
Fuel tank: 9.5 litres

Performance:
Top speed: 80 km/h
Fuel consumption: 2.8 l/100 km

Features: Handlebar fairing.

Manufacturer: Tovarna Motornih Vozil Tomos – Smarska cesta 4,
66001 Koper, Yugoslavia.

TOMOS (Yugoslavia)

Model: ATX50

Engine: 2-str single
Capacity: 49 cc
Bore × Stroke: 38 × 43 mm
Compression ratio: 7:1
Carburettor: ...
Maximum power: 1.6 bhp at
5 500 rpm
Starting: kick

Transmission: 5-speed chain

Electrics: 12 v magneto ignition

Frame: Tubular spine

Suspension: Telescopic front
fork with twin oil/spring rear
dampers.

Brakes: 105 mm drums
front and rear

Tyres: Front is 2.50–18
Rear is 2.75–18

Dimensions:
Length: 1 860 mm
Width: ...
Wheelbase: ...
Clearance: ...
Seat height: ...
Dry weight: 70 kg
Fuel tank: 9.5 litres

Performance:
Top speed: 50 km/h
Fuel consumption: 2.1 l/100 km

Features: Dual purpose bike.

Manufacturer: Tovarna Motornih Vozil.

TRIUMPH (England)

Model: Bonneville UK

Engine: 4-str ohv
parallel twin
Capacity: 744 cc
Bore × Stroke: 76 × 82 mm
Compression ratio: 7.9:1
Carburettor: 2 × 30 mm Amal
Maximum power: 50 bhp at
7 200 rpm
Starting: kick

Transmission: 5-speed chain

Electrics: 12 v electronic
ignition with 8 Ah battery

Frame: Steel double cradle

Suspension: Telehydraulic
front fork with twin rear
hydraulic dampers.

Brakes: 260 mm triple disc
system

Tyres: Front is 100/90H19
Rear is 110/90H18

Dimensions:
Length: 2 200 mm
Width: 686 mm
Wheelbase: 1 422 mm
Clearance: 180 mm
Seat height: 787 mm
Dry weight: 186 kg
Fuel tank: 18.2 litres

Performance:
Top speed: 180 km/h
Fuel consumption: 5.6 l/100 km

Features: USA version has
smaller 13 litres tank.

Manufacturer: L. F. Harris (Rushden) Ltd, Units 1 & 2 Silverhills
Road, Decoy Industrial Estate, Newton Abbot, Devon TQ12 5ND,
England.

YAMAHA (Japan)

Model: XVZ12TD Venture

Engine: 4-str dohc 16-valve
LC vee-four
Capacity: 1 198 cc
Bore × Stroke: 76 × 66 mm
Compression ratio: 10.5:1
Carburettor: 4 × 34 mm Mikuni
Maximum power: 97 bhp at
7 000 rpm
Starting: electric

Transmission: 5-speed shaft
drive

Electrics: 12 v electronic
ignition with 20 Ah battery

Frame: Steel tubular cradle

Suspension: Air-assisted front
fork with rear 4-way adjustable
Monocross.

Brakes: Triple 282 mm disc
system with linked braking

Tyres: Front is 120/90H18
Rear is 140/90H18

Dimensions:
Length: 2 470 mm
Width: 920 mm
Wheelbase: 1 610 mm
Clearance: 145 mm
Seat height: 785 mm
Dry weight: 321 kg
Fuel tank: 20 litres

Performance:
Top speed: 190 km/h
Fuel consumption: 7 l/100 km

Features: Full-dress tourer
with stereo radio and cassette.

Manufacturer: Yamaha Motor Co. Ltd, Shizuoka-ken, PO Box 1,
Iwata, Japan.

YAMAHA (Japan)

Model: FJ1200

Engine: 4-str dohc 16-valve in-line four
Capacity: 1 188 cc
Bore × Stroke: 77 × 63.8 mm
Compression ratio: 9.7:1
Carburettor: 4 × 36 mm Mikuni
Maximum power: 125 bhp at 9 000 rpm
Starting: electric

Transmission: 5-speed chain

Electrics: 12 v electronic ignition with 14 Ah battery

Frame: Genesis box section cradle

Suspension: Telescopic front fork with adjustable anti-dive and single rear gas/oil *Monocross* system.

Brakes: 282 mm triple disc system

Tyres: Front is 120/80V16
Rear is 150/80V16

Dimensions:
Length: 2 230 mm
Width: 775 mm
Wheelbase: 1 490 mm
Clearance: 140 mm
Seat height: 780 mm
Dry weight: 236 kg
Fuel tank: 22 litres

Performance:
Top speed: 240 km/h
Fuel consumption: 7 l/100 km

Features: Fairing windshield options – sports low, touring high. Stainless steel exhaust, flush-fitting alloy fuel filler.

Manufacturer: Yamaha Motor Co. Ltd.

YAMAHA (Japan)

Model: FZR1000

Engine: 4-str dohc 20-valve
LC parallel four
Capacity: 989 cc
Bore × Stroke: 75 × 56 mm
Compression ratio: 11.2:1
Carburettor: 4 × 37 mm cv
Mikuni
Maximum power: 125 bhp at
10 000 rpm
Starting: electric

Transmission: 5-speed chain

Electrics: 12 v digital ignition
with 14 Ah battery

Frame: Aluminium Deltabox

Suspension: Telescopic front
fork with *Monocross* rear using
gas/oil De Carbon-type dampers.

Brakes: Twin floating 320 mm
discs with 267 mm rear disc

Tyres: Front is 120/70V17
Rear is 160/60V18

Dimensions:
Length: 2 205 mm
Width: 730 mm
Wheelbase: 1 215 mm
Clearance: 140 mm
Seat height: 775 mm
Dry weight: 204 kg
Fuel tank: 20 litres

Performance:
Top speed: 260 km/h
Fuel consumption: 8.6 l/100 km

Features: 5 valves per cylinder,
opposed-piston caliper braking
power, 4-into-1 stainless steel
exhaust with racing bean can,
cast alloy wheels and twin
halogen headlights.

Manufacturer: Yamaha Motor Co. Ltd.

YAMAHA (Japan)

Model: XV1000SE Virago

Engine: 4-str sohc 75° vee-twin
Capacity: 981 cc
Bore × Stroke: 95 × 69.2 mm
Compression ratio: 8.3:1
Carburettor: 2 × 40 mm cv
Hitachi
Maximum power: 63.5 bhp at
6 500 rpm
Starting: electric

Transmission: 5-speed shaft
drive

Electrics: 12 v electronic
ignition with 14 Ah battery

Frame: Monocoque beam
chassis

Suspension: Telescopic air-
assisted front fork with twin 4-
way adjustable rear dampers.

Manufacturer: Yamaha Motor Co. Ltd.

Brakes: 267 mm slotted twin
disc with rear drum

Tyres: Front is 100/90H19
Rear is 140/90H15

Dimensions:
Length: 2 235 mm
Width: 840 mm
Wheelbase: 1 525 mm
Clearance: 145 mm
Seat height: 715 mm
Dry weight: 220 kg
Fuel tank: 14.5 litres

Performance:
Top speed: 180 km
Fuel consumption: 5.5 l/100 km

Features: Custom styling with
chromed shorty silencers, back
rest and grab bar, black 'glove
leather' upholstery, side and
centre stands.

YAMAHA (Japan)

Model: XJ900F

Engine: 4-str dohc YICS
parallel four
Capacity: 891 cc
Bore × Stroke: 68.5 × 60.5 mm
Compression ratio: 9.6:1
Carburettor: 4 × 36 mm Mikuni
Maximum power: 98 bhp at
9 000 rpm
Starting: electric

Transmission: 5-speed shaft
drive

Electrics: 12 v electronic
ignition with 14 Ah battery

Frame: Duplex tubular cradle

Suspension: Air-assisted front
fork with twin rear adjustable
dampers.

Brakes: 235 mm triple slotted
disc system with opposed piston
calipers

Tyres: Front is 100/90V18
Rear is 120/90V18

Dimensions:
Length: 2 215 mm
Width: 735 mm
Wheelbase: 1 480 mm
Clearance: 145 mm
Seat height: 780 mm
Dry weight: 218 kg
Fuel tank: 22 litres

Performance:
Top speed: 210 km/h
Fuel consumption: 6.6 l/100 km

Features: Yamaha Induction
Control System for combustion
efficiency. Oil cooler, frame-
mounted head fairing, cast alloy
wheels, digital clock.

Manufacturer: Yamaha Motor Co. Ltd.

YAMAHA (Japan)

Model: FZX750

Engine: 4-str dohc 20-valve
LC parallel four
Capacity: 749 cc
Bore × Stroke: 68 × 51.6 mm
Compression ratio: 11.2:1
Carburettor: 4 × 34 mm Mikuni
Maximum power: 107 bhp at
10 500 rpm
Starting: electric

Transmission: 6-speed chain

Electrics: 12 v digital ignition
with 14 Ah battery

Frame: Box section steel cradle

Suspension: Air-assisted front
fork with adjustable *Monocross*
system.

Brakes: Ventilated triple
210 mm disc system with
opposed piston calipers

Tyres: Front is 120/80V16
Rear is 130/80V18

Dimensions:
Length: 2 230 mm
Width: 755 mm
Wheelbase: 1 490 mm
Clearance: 145 mm
Seat height: 800 mm
Dry weight: 205 kg
Fuel tank: 21 litres

Performance:
Top speed: 235 km/h
Fuel consumption: 6 l/100 km

Features: Genesis concept
race proved design, full fairing, 4-
into-1 bean can exhaust, race
type seat cowl, Electric cooling
fan.

Manufacturer: Yamaha Motor Co. Ltd.

YAMAHA (Japan)

Model: FZX750 Fazer

Engine: 4-str dohc 20-valve LC parallel four inclined at 45°
Capacity: 749 cc
Bore × Stroke: 68 × 51.6 mm
Compression ratio: 11.2:1
Carburettor: 4 × 34 mm Mikuni
Maximum power: 94 bhp at 9 500 rpm
Starting: electric

Transmission: 6-speed chain

Electrics: 12 v electronic ignition with 14 Ah battery

Frame: Steel box section cradle

Suspension: Air-assisted front fork with twin De Carbon gas dampers.

Brakes: 267 mm triple slotted disc system with opposed piston calipers

Tyres: Front is 110/90V16
Rear is 140/90V15

Dimensions:
Length: 2 245 mm
Width: 785 mm
Wheelbase: 1 525 mm
Clearance: 150 mm
Seat height: 750 mm
Dry weight: 204 kg
Fuel tank: 13 litres

Performance:
Top speed: 210 km/h
Fuel consumption: 5.8 l/100 km

Features: Street cruiser concept, Genesis layout, chrome-plated 4-into-2 exhaust system, aluminium dish wheels.

Manufacturer: Yamaha Motor Co. Ltd.

YAMAHA (Japan)

Model: SRX600

Engine: 4-str sohc
4-valve single
Capacity: 608 cc
Bore × Stroke: 96 × 84 mm
Compression ratio: 8.5:1
Carburettor: 27 mm Mikuni
Maximum power: 45 bhp at
6 500 rpm
Starting: kick

Transmission: 5-speed sealed
chain

Electrics: 12 v CDI ignition

Frame: Double cradle box
section

Suspension: Telescopic front
fork and twin rear dampers.

Manufacturer: Yamaha Motor Co. Ltd.

Brakes: Triple slotted discs
with opposed piston calipers

Tyres: Front is 100/80-18
Rear is 128/80-16

Dimensions:
Length: 2 085 mm
Width: 705 mm
Wheelbase: 1 385 mm
Clearance: 145 mm
Seat height: 770 mm
Dry weight: 149 kg
Fuel tank: 15 litres

Performance:
Top speed: 175 km/h
Fuel consumption: 5.8 l/100 km

Features: Aluminium oil tank
and side panels, dry sump
lubrication.

YAMAHA (Japan)

Model: FZ600

Engine: 4-str dohc parallel four
Capacity: 598 cc
Bore × Stroke: 58.5 × 55.7 mm
Compression ratio: 10:1
Carburettor: 4 × 30 mm cv
Mikuni
Maximum power: 69.2 bhp at
9 500 rpm
Starting: electric

Transmission: 6-speed 'O' ring
chain

Electrics: 12 v electronic
ignition with 12 Ah battery

Frame: Steel box section cradle

Suspension: Air-assisted front
fork with 5-position remote
adjustment *Monocross* system.

Brakes: Triple slotted disc
system – opposed piston calipers

Tyres: Front is 100/90H16
Rear is 120/80H18

Dimensions:
Length: 2 025 mm
Width: 690 mm
Wheelbase: 1 385 mm
Clearance: 135 mm
Seat height: 785 mm
Dry weight: 186 kg
Fuel tank: 16 litres

Performance:
Top speed: 200 km/h
Fuel consumption: 5.5 l/100 km

Features: Race replica looks
with slippery aerodynamics, one
piece, racing style lightweight
exhaust, flush fitting fuel cap,
side stand.

Manufacturer: Yamaha Motor Co. Ltd.

YAMAHA (Japan)

Model: XT600

Engine: 4-str sohc 4-valve
single with Yamaha Duo Intake
System
Capacity: 595 cc
Bore × Stroke: 95 × 84 mm
Compression ratio: 8.5:1
Carburettor: 27 mm twin choke
type
Maximum power: 45 bhp at
6 500 rpm
Starting: kick

Transmission: 5-speed chain

Electrics: 12 v CDI ignition
with 5 Ah battery

Frame: Tubular diamond cradle

Suspension: Telescopic front
fork with rising rate *Monocross*
system.

Manufacturer: Yamaha Motor Co. Ltd.

Brakes: 220 mm single discs
front and rear with floating alloy
calipers

Tyres: Front is 3.00S21
Rear is 4.60S18

Dimensions:
Length: 2 210 mm
Width: 885 mm
Wheelbase: 1 440 mm
Clearance: 265 mm
Seat height: 885 mm
Dry weight: 140 kg
Fuel tank: 13 litres

Performance:
Top speed: 160 km/h
Fuel consumption: 5.6 l/100 km

Features: Motorcross style
seat and stash bag. Tenere is
Paris-Dakar Rally replica with 23
litre pannier fuel tank and
electric start.

YAMAHA (Japan)

Model: RD350F

Engine: 2-str reed-valve LC
YPVS twin
Capacity: 347 cc
Bore × Stroke: 64 × 54 mm
Compression ratio: 6:1
Carburettor: 2 × 26 mm Mikuni
Maximum power: 63 bhp at
9 000 rpm
Starting: kick

Transmission: 6-speed chain

Electrics: 12 v CDI ignition
with 5 Ah battery

Frame: Tubular wide-cradle,
fully triangulated

Suspension: Air-assisted front
fork with De Carbon-type
Monocross system.

Brakes: 267 mm slotted triple
disc system with opposing
piston calipers

Tyres: Front is 90/90H18
Rear is 100/80H18

Dimensions:
Length: 2 095 mm
Width: 700 mm
Wheelbase: 1 190 mm
Clearance: 165 mm
Seat height: 790 mm
Dry weight: 141 kg
Fuel tank: 17 litres

Performance:
Top speed: 195 km/h
Fuel consumption: 7 l/100 km

Features: Yamaha Power
Valve System to give
smoothness across the rev range,
racing type bean can exhaust
and frame-fitted fairing.
Available as RD350 without
fairing.

Manufacturer: Yamaha Motor Co. Ltd.

YAMAHA (Japan)

Model: TZR250

Engine: 2-str reed-valve LC YPVS parallel twin
Capacity: 249 cc
Bore × Stroke: 56.4 × 50 mm
Compression ratio: 5.9:1
Carburettor: 2 × 28 mm flat-slide Mikuni
Maximum power: 50 bhp at 10 000 rpm
Starting: kick

Transmission: 6-speed chain

Electrics: 12 v CDI ignition

Frame: Aluminium Delta Box

Suspension: Air-assisted front fork with De Carbon type rising rate *Monocross* at rear.

Brakes: 320 mm drilled floating disc with opposed pistons and 210 mm rear disc

Tyres: Front is 100/80H17
Rear is 120/80H17

Dimensions:
Length: 2 040 mm
Width: 660 mm
Wheelbase: 1 135 mm
Clearance: 135 mm
Seat height: 760 mm
Dry weight: 128 kg
Fuel tank: 16 litres

Performance:
Top speed: 190 km/h
Fuel consumption: 7 l/100 km

Features: Aerodynamic full fairing, hollow-spoke, cast alloy wheels, racer-styled instrument panel, and track-developed exhaust system.

Manufacturer: Yamaha Motor Co. Ltd.

YAMAHA (Japan)

Model: TZR125

Engine: 2-str reed-valve LC
YEIS single
Capacity: 124 cc
Bore × Stroke: 56.4 × 50 mm
Compression ratio: 5.9:1
Carburettor: 26 mm Mikuni
Maximum power: 12.2 bhp at
7 500 rpm
Starting: kick

Transmission: 6-speed chain

Electrics: 12 v CDI ignition
with 5 Ah battery

Frame: Steel-pressed Delta Box

Suspension: Telescopic front
fork with rear *Monocross* system.

Brakes: Slotted 245 mm front
disc and rear drum

Tyres: Front is 90/90-16
Rear is 100/90-18

Dimensions:
Length: 2 020 mm
Width: 695 mm
Wheelbase: 1 340 mm
Clearance: 135 mm
Seat height: 760 mm
Dry weight: 108 kg
Fuel tank: 12 litres

Performance:
Top speed: 120 km/h
Fuel consumption: 5.8 l/100 km

Features: TZ road racer
pedigree, optional full fairing,
Yamaha Energy Induction
System boosts pulling power
and helps fuel economy.
European models have Power
Valve fitted.

Manufacturer: Yamaha Motor Co. Ltd.

YAMAHA (Japan)

Model: RDZ125LC

Engine: 2-str reed-valve
LC single
Capacity: 123 cc
Bore × Stroke: 56 × 50 mm
Compression ratio: 6.4:1
Carburettor: 24 mm Mikuni
Maximum power: 12.2 bhp at
7 500 rpm
Starting: kick

Transmission: 6-speed chain

Electrics: 12 v CDI ignition
with 5 Ah battery

Frame: Steel tubular cradle

Suspension: Telescopic front
fork with adjustable rear
Monocross system.

Manufacturer: Yamaha Motor Co. Ltd.

Brakes: 245 mm front disc and
130 mm rear drum

Tyres: Front is 80/100-16
Rear is 90/90-18

Dimensions:
Length: 1 940 mm
Width: 695 mm
Wheelbase: 1 275 mm
Clearance: 165 mm
Seat height: 755 mm
Dry weight: 98 kg
Fuel tank: 13 litres

Performance:
Top speed: 120 km/h
Fuel consumption: 4.5 l/100 km

Features: Handlebar fairing.
Fixed power valve engine. Cast
alloy wheels. Grab handle.

YAMAHA (Japan)

Model: DT125LC

Engine: 2-str reed-valve YEIS
single
Capacity: 123 cc
Bore × Stroke: 56 × 50 mm
Compression ratio: 6.8:1
Carburettor: 26 mm PowerJet
Mikuni
Maximum power: 12.2 bhp at
6 500 rpm
Starting: kick

Transmission: 6-speed O ring
chain

Electrics: 12 v CDI ignition

Frame: Tubular cradle

Suspension: Leading axle front
fork with rising-rate *Monocross*
at rear.

Brakes: Drilled front disc with
plastic mudshield and rear drum

Tyres: Front is 2.75-21
Rear is 4.10-18

Dimensions:
Length: 2 140 mm
Width: 820 mm
Wheelbase: 1 360 mm
Clearance: 285 mm
Seat height: 845 mm
Dry weight: 99 kg
Fuel tank: 10 litres

Performance:
Top speed: 105 km/h
Fuel consumption: 5 l/100 km

Features: Sporting trail bike
with motorcrosser features.
Plastic used for front fender and
engine guard. Range includes a
DT50MX.

Manufacturer: Yamaha Motor Co. Ltd.

YAMAHA (Japan)

Model: YB100

Engine: 2-str rotary-valve single
Capacity: 97 cc
Bore × Stroke: 52 × 45.6 mm
Compression ratio: 6.5:1
Carburettor: 20 mm Mikuni
Maximum power: 9.8 bhp at
8 000 rpm
Starting: kick

Transmission: 4-speed
enclosed chain

Electrics: 6 v flywheel magneto

Frame: Pressed steel spine

Suspension: Telescopic front
fork with twin rear hydraulic
dampers.

Manufacturer: Yamaha Motor Co. Ltd.

Brakes: 110 mm labyrinth seal
drums front and rear

Tyres: 2.50-18 front and rear

Dimensions:
Length: 1 850 mm
Width: 735 mm
Wheelbase: 1 180 mm
Clearance: 140 mm
Seat height: 785 mm
Dry weight: 84 kg
Fuel tank: 8.6 litres

Performance:
Top speed: 104 km/h
Fuel consumption: 3.2 l/100 km

Features: Autolube oil
injection.

YAMAHA (Japan)

Model: T80 Town Mate

Engine: 4-str sohc single
Capacity: 79 cc
Bore × Stroke: 47 × 45.6 mm
Compression ratio: 9.6:1
Carburettor: 16 mm Mikuni
Maximum power: 6.5 bhp at
7 500 rpm
Starting: kick

Transmission: 4-speed
automatic shaft drive

Electrics: 12 v CDI ignition

Frame: Step-thru pressed steel

Suspension: Leading link fork
with twin hydraulic dampers.

Brakes: 110 mm drums front
and rear

Tyres: 2.50-17 front and rear

Dimensions:
Length: 1 860 mm
Width: 670 mm
Wheelbase: 1 050 mm
Clearance: 130 mm
Seat height: 750 mm
Dry weight: 81 kg
Fuel tank: 8.5 litres

Performance:
Top speed: 93 km/h
Fuel consumption: 1.5 l/100 km

Features: Fuel gauge,
legshields. 3-speed T50 version.
Autolube.

Manufacturer: Yamaha Motor Co. Ltd.

YAMAHA (Japan)

Model: FS1

Engine: 2-str rotary-valve single
Capacity: 49 cc
Bore × Stroke: 40 × 39.7 mm
Compression ratio: 6.6:1
Carburettor: 16 mm Mikuni
Maximum power: 2.95 bhp at
5 000 rpm
Starting: kick

Transmission: 4-speed chain

Electrics: 6 v flywheel magneto

Frame: Tubular cradle

Suspension: Hydraulic front
fork with twin rear dampers.

Brakes: Labyrinth seal drums
front and rear

Tyres: 2.50-17 front and rear

Dimensions:
Length: 1 825 mm
Width: 750 mm
Wheelbase: 1 160 mm
Clearance: 145 mm
Seat height: 780 mm
Dry weight: 72 kg
Fuel tank: 9 litres

Performance:
Top speed: 48 km/h
Fuel consumption: 3 l/100 km

Features: Autolube oil
injection. Long-running sports
moped with full motorbike
features.

Manufacturer: Yamaha Motor Co. Ltd.

YAMAHA (Japan)

Model: QT50

Engine: 2-str single
Capacity: 49 cc
Bore × Stroke: 40 × 39.2 mm
Compression ratio: 5.9:1
Carburettor: 12 mm Mikuni
Maximum power: 2.3 bhp at
5 500 rpm
Starting: kick

Transmission: Shaft drive
automatic

Electrics: 12 v CDI ignition

Frame: Lightweight step-thru

Suspension: Leading link fork
and single rear damper.

Brakes: Drums front and rear

Tyres: Front is 2.00-14
Rear is 2.25-14

Dimensions:
Length: 1 545 mm
Width: 660 mm
Wheelbase: 1 050 mm
Clearance: 110 mm
Seat height: 715 mm
Dry weight: 45 kg
Fuel tank: 2.3 litres

Performance:
Top speed: 48 km/h
Fuel consumption: 1.5 l/100 km

Features: Autolube oil
injection, rear luggage rack and
front shopping basket,
legshields.

Manufacturer: Yamaha Motor Co. Ltd.

YAMAHA (Japan)

Model: JOG

Engine: 2-str reed-valve
fan-cooled single
Capacity: 49 cc
Bore × Stroke: 40 × 39.2 mm
Compression ratio: 7:1
Carburettor: 12 mm Mikuni
Maximum power: 3.9 bhp at
6 500 rpm
Starting: electric/kick

Transmission: Fully automatic
belt drive

Electrics: 12 v CDI ignition

Frame: Monocoque

Suspension: Telescopic front
fork with rear monoshock system.

Manufacturer: Yamaha Motor Co. Ltd.

Brakes: Drums front and rear

Tyres: 3.00-10 front and rear

Dimensions:
Length: 1 610 mm
Width: 625 mm
Wheelbase: 1 115 mm
Clearance: 95 mm
Seat height: 690 mm
Dry weight: 58 kg
Fuel tank: 3.5 litres

Performance:
Top speed: 48 km/h
Fuel consumption: 2 l/100 km

Features: Rubber-mounted
engine. Rear rack.